C000277308

BINARY MYTHS 1 & 2

– Stride –

BINARY MYTHS 1 & 2

edited by
Andy Brown

BINARY MYTHS 1 & 2
New edition 2004
© 2004

Selection and Introduction
© Andy Brown

ISBN 1 900152 96 7

Cover photo by Rupert Loydell
Cover design by Neil Annat

Acknowledgements
Part of the introduction was first published
as a critical essay in *Scratch* 17.
Binary Myths was originally published by Stride in 1998.
Binary Myths 2 was originally published by Stride in 1999.

Published by
Stride Publications
11 Sylvan Road, Exeter
Devon EX4 6EW

www.stridebooks.co.uk

Contents

BINARY MYTHS

conversations with contemporary poets

Introduction

Many of the concerns and questions publically voiced in contemporary poetry seem to be ones which have long been addressed in other art-forms – those of the relative values of Form vs. Abstraction; Accessibility vs. Difficulty; Music vs. Meaning, and so on. Why are poets and critics still thrashing this one out, when the visual arts and music, in particular, seem to have gone far beyond many of the questions raised by the critical theories of this century? Certain areas of poetry are still stuck in the debates and binary myths of old: Populism vs. Modernism; Everyman vs. the Elitist.

In a review of *The New Poetry*, Andrew Duncan (*Angel Exhaust Eleven*) asks the important question

Does the avant garde have a separate discourse any more?

equating much experimental work with a similar style of

...disapproval, diffidence, wit, embarrassment...

that he detects in many of *The New Poetry*'s writers. Peter Finch reiterates the question in a recent article (*Writers' Monthly*, August '96):

Is 'avant garde' a reasonable term to use when describing poetry?

Finch also points out how 'Critics despise the stuff', going on to ask what is probably the more-often voiced question: 'How does anyone get a handle?' It is also worth noting the tone of resignation in Finch's closing remarks:

The avant garde and the regular do not make a habit of mixing, no matter how advantageous it might be if they did.

Sadly true maybe, but why don't they mix and in what ways might it be advantageous if they did? When faced with the same contemporary problems, what are the areas of dialogue; the differences and discrepancies? Do these polarities in fact exist? And if it turns out that there isn't a shared ground or area of dialogue, does that mean we have to inevitably slip into the petty sniping and sidelining that so much contemporary criticism passes as?

Much has been written and said about *The New Poetry* anthology and the New Generation Poets promotion, just or unjust, constructive or diatribe, depending on your taste and point of view. Whatever, it has little to do with progressive dialogue, but continues slotting poets into neatly defined groups that serve no ends other than those of marketing men, poetry anthology editors, or academics.

Considering some of the binary oppositions that are set up in contemporary poetry, what is supposedly missing in the Everyman Populism of much of our higher-profile contemporary poetry, with its overt accessibility? Allegedly, it might be issues of Identity, Language, Philosophy, Culture and Politics, no doubt central to our late Twentieth Century experience. Within this poetry, these elements are seemingly overwhelmed by the need to convince the reading public that poetry is 'The New Rock'n'Roll'. Conversely, the writing, publishing and/or performance of 'the innovative text' raises problematic questions with the populist poets, primarily on the grounds that innovative texts are difficult / elitist or (more paradoxically) that 'difficult' texts are in fact *easy to write*. It is within this narrow frame of argument that the populist cannot appreciate a 'difficult' text, because it is 'elitist', or just 'plain bad writing'; and the linguistically-innovative poet cannot appreciate a 'populist' poem, because it is 'simplistic', or just 'plain bad writing'.

A recent claim for bringing 'difficulty' back into poetry, is to be found in Iain Sinclair's introduction to the anthology *The Conductors Of Chaos* (Picador, 1996):

> Why should they be easy? Why should they not reflect some measure of the complexity of the climate in which they exist ?

Conversely, aggressive reviewers have also slammed the anthology, finding it:

> ...wallowing humourlessly in randomness and arbitrariness...the half-assed splenetic sloppiness to which this book stands testament...any half-way decent computer programmer could do the same.
> *The Oxford Quarterly*, Vol 1 No 4

There it is again, the 'anyone can do it' mentality that excuses itself as constructive criticism; the kind of uncritical slanging match that editing and criticising anthologies has become – part and parcel of the gamesmanship and patriarchal ennui of 'The Anthology Wars'.

Which brings me back to a central theme of this book and the one basic problem upon which this hinges – all of us use language, stake our claims upon it and personalize it beyond the belief of others, when we haven't really come to any kind of consensus on what poetry is; what and who it is for; what it is capable of and how we can discuss that *in language* with others. Those questions seem to have been left to those working in marketing departments and a select handful of poetry editors. What really troubles me in all of this is, not that poetry is marketed but, that poets themselves begin to believe the marketing claims of their publishers, or poetry circles, whether they be 'mainstream' or 'avant garde'; that the commercial and intellectual manipulation of 'brand names' of poetry forms the framework into which poets become slotted / slot themselves, and in which the 'value' of poetry is discussed. As to whether there is anything in the perception of a divided writing community, the poets must speak for themselves.

Rather than adopt a formal interview approach, this project was conducted through correspondence, giving each of the writers the chance to answer the same or similar questions, or to choose from them the areas of enquiry which were of most interest. I submitted the same collection of questions to each writer, inviting answers to a question from each thematic section, as well as inviting each writer to contribute some areas of discussion they were particularly interested in, though not all did so. After their initial responses, we continued the correspondence to pick up on recurring themes, or to explore emerging avenues of enquiry. The writers have all engaged in these interviews with candour and enthusiasm and I am deeply grateful to them all for their interest and support and would like to extend my warmest thanks. Many of the questions inevitably set up binary oppositions – the exact kind I have been arguing against in this introduction – with the aim of inviting deconstructive comment by the poets; with the aim of doing away with the kind of either-ors, the binary myths, that stifle poetic practice and comment.

Andy Brown, 1996

David Kennedy

Should poetry be difficult? Does 'popular' necessarily mean 'simple'?

There's been a tremendous amount of anxious discussion of these questions post-*The New Poetry* and particularly post-New Generation Poets. Peter Forbes even went so far as to assert in *Poetry Review* that increasing numbers of poets are writing in what he called the New Plain Style. I think it's significant that this anxiety about readership is inextricable from the so-called 'poetry boom' and this suggests that the anxiety is to a large degree economic. More poets are writing and publishing than ever before and so need to create a larger market for their products. And yet it would be hard to argue that there's a significantly larger audience for poetry – just look at the size of the poetry section in the average Blackwell's or W.H. Smith's. The American critic Joseph Epstein caught the situation rather well when he wrote at the end of the 1980s that 'contemporary poetry has not grown more but less difficult, and the audience still isn't there'. In this context, questions of popularity become irrelevant.

My own belief is that poetry should be 'difficult' in the sense that it should deal with difficulty. Take, for example, Tony Harrison's sonnet 'Classics Society'. Here are sixteen lines of rhymed verse which deal with, among other things, the working-class experience of improved access to education in the post-war period; the way a nation exercises cultural and political hegemony through educational and linguistic standards; and the way culture moulds individual experience into a bourgeois discourse. The poem is a unified and satisfying work of art which at the same time causes the reader to reflect on his or her privilege at being able to appreciate its complexity and, consequently, those excluded from that privilege. What other cultural genre could cover so much ground in so small a space? I believe that poetry should also be difficult in the sense that John Ashbery is 'difficult'. Again, I'd like to quote an American critic to underline what I mean. (There seem to be few, if any, English critics writing about these sorts of questions.) Vernon Shelley writes in his book *After The Death of Poetry: Poet and Audience in Contemporary America* that poetry is uniquely placed

> to record the form and pressure of the time upon consciousness. But given that our era is one dominated, intellectually, by various radical scepticisms, that recording must itself show the mark of those scepticisms, must itself demonstrate the poet's awareness of the corrosive doubt about the nature of subjectivity itself that thinking people now inhabit

[...] only poetry can tell us how living with and in that doubt affects the nature of our feelings.

Of course, this rather assumes that poets are thinking people; the level of discourse about poetry in even our leading poetry magazines contributes to a corrosive doubt about that.

What's going on in contemporary poetry that interests you?

The British poets whose work excites me – poets such as John Ash, Robert Crawford, Peter Didsbury, Ian Duhig, Roy Fisher, Maggie Hannan, Sean O'Brien, Deryn Rees-Jones, Denise Riley, Jo Shapcott and John Hartley-Williams – can be said to be writing against the kind of world view anatomised by Andrew Duncan in *Angel Exhaust Eleven*: 'The position is: *I don't feel sexual desire; I don't understand the situation; I have no pretensions to culture;* [...] It follows that: *I have nothing of interest to say; I am lying.*' What the work of these writers has in common is an interest in poetry as a cultural genre uniquely placed for the staging and exploring of difficulty, of matters arising from questions of discourse, gender, history, politics and sexuality. Poems, their work seems to be saying, are not just containers for confession, expression, or observation, but kinds of machine, difference engines which explore the play of differences anew each time they are written and read. This play of differences means that their work relishes combining elements of the mainstream and the avant garde: surrealism with naturalism or realism with postmodernism. This 'mix' or sampling, this interest in versions as opposed to final texts, seems to me to be fundamental to culture and, indeed, to things in general at this late point in the century. It's what the poet Ian Gregson calls 'mingledness'. This means, for example, that it's not a case of being able to say definitively that the British poetry renaissance of the 1980s and 1990s is the result of either a kind of post-colonialism internal to the British Isles in which the margins write back to the centre, *or* of New Right free market 'Big Bang' in poetry publishing, but of having to come to terms with the discomfiting reality that both things are true. In terms of poetic practice, poetry is not a choice between ellipsis and parataxis *or* metaphor and simile, but a recognition that not only are all four valuable strategies, but that none are either exclusively avant garde or exclusively mainstream.

What social / political interests motivate your writing, if any?

Eliot says somewhere that there aren't any new emotions and that attempts to describe any are just discussions of perversity, but I think there *are* feelings that are peculiar to the way we live now. It's these that I'm interested in exploring in my poetry. You might say all these feelings arise from the uncomfortable awareness we have that destiny has been replaced by choice. I'm working on a sequence at the moment called 'Postmodern Scenes'. I think I can best illustrate what I mean by referring to the opening page of a novel called *The Primitive* by Stephen Amidon. The protagonist, David Webster, is racing down a mountain road having 'slotted the gear stick into neutral several miles back, content to let gravity fuel his descent.' Halfway down, he passes a truck escape lane: 'For an instant David pictured himself in that position, brakeless and forced to choose.' Here we have someone in control of a powerful machine, in absolutely no danger at all and yet part of the enjoyment of the control is his fantasy of its opposite. Another example of the feelings I'm talking about would be a common sight in cities, namely a group of people standing around watching a building being pulled down. It's as if they're passive observers of change, but intimately involved in it too. It's as if they're watching profound changes to their world as a kind of entertainment. My other great interest is England and 'Englishness'. The critic David Gervais says that our England is actually 'the aftermath of England' and I'm interested in exploring that condition. My work is very similar to Sean O'Brien's in this area, but where his work is often animated by a genuine political anger, I'm more interested in a kind of cultural archaeology. There's a comment by Douglas Dunn that sums up my view of the function of poetry: 'When poetry ceases to be civilization-making, it becomes smugly minor, 'interesting', decorative and self-satisfied. To be other than that in our own times means risking a poetry that will be criticising.' I think poetry has to take that risk if it is to retain its readership and, indeed, any credibility as a genre.

Have you collaborated with other artists / writers on any work recently? How has this developed your poetry?

For the past two years I've been collaborating with the poet and translator Christopher Pilling on versions of prose poems from Max Jacob's surrealist classic of 1914 *Le Cornet à Dés* (The Dice Cup), which will be published later this year [1996] by Atlas. I think translation is an excellent way of keeping yourself in shape as a poet. I always find I write much better afterwards. It concentrates you on matters of style and unity, in the sense that Flaubert meant and in the detached manner that he insisted was so important. In fact, translation, particularly for a poet, is an excellent way of avoiding the temptations of all those ideas of poetry as self-expression. Translation is a way of learning to think.

I think collaboration is tremendously important for poets. We don't get a lot of opportunity to do it – 'moonlit garret' models of creation are still far too prevalent – and creativity only truly functions through relationships. I always find collaboration is a lot of fun and huge amounts of energy and excitement seem to get released which perhaps wouldn't otherwise.

What processes lie behind the writing of your poems? What kind of sources / source materials do you like to use?

I always identify myself as a poet and critic, because for me the two activities are seamless. When I sit down to write I often don't know whether it's a poem or a critical piece that's going to be produced. For example, similar ideas appear in my group of poems about Englishness 'Looking For England' and in a conference paper I gave recently about the presence of the past in the work of Sean O'Brien and Patrick McGrath. I'm very attracted to and excited by this sort of slippage between different discourses. I'm rather distrustful of the idea of 'voice' which seems to me to be used in rather woolly and misleading senses. I think Muldoon has it right when he says (of his own creative writing teaching) that he encourages his students to try to 'allow themselves to be taken over by the possibilities of language' and to be '*humble*, as it were, before language'. I think, too, that there needs to be greater emphasis in teaching on the discursive as opposed to the expressive.

I also work with cut-up techniques a lot. My Scratch pamphlet *The Elephant's Typewriter* contains 12 sixteen line poems from a sequence of 50 which were composed by combining found material, old notebooks and free writing between them. I like to start with the real or the naturalistic and then play around with it, kind of float free of it. The sequence itself was generated within a structure formed by the last line of one poem becoming the first line of the next. Similarly, I recently wrote a poem which cut-up a report I found on the Internet from one of the space shuttle astronauts. I suppose all this is a way of saying that I usually start with an idea as opposed to an observation taken from life. I'm really not interested in producing poems that are like photographs or family memoirs.

To what extent should poets be concerned with the age in which they are living?

I suppose I would want to ask what other age poets should be concerned with! I argue with Robert Crawford's comment that 'Directly or obliquely, a good poem is faithful to the language of its age. If it sounds unidiomatic, it sinks', so I find it impossible to conceive of any other answer than 'totally'. This is why I think Jo Shapcott's *Phrasebook* is one of the most important poems of recent years. I tried to make this point with a different emphasis in the review of *Emergency Kit* I wrote for *Poetry Review* by quoting from Susan Rubin Sulieman's book *Risking Who One Is*. In her introduction, Sulieman writes about the difficulties involved in being a critic of the contemporary, but I think her ideas apply equally well to the contemporary creative artist. She talks about what she calls 'intersection' with other people and their lives, the sense that 'for a number of years we breathed the same air and participated in at least some aspects of the same material culture'. Now, it seems to me that one can read large quantities of contemporary English poetry and get absolutely no sense of 'intersection' at all. In contrast, what makes contemporary Australian poetry so exciting is *precisely* this: it's not just that John Tranter or John Forbes have poems about cars and driving and television, but that their work is animated by a powerful sense of the self as an economic self and a consuming self. They wonder what happens to democracy when we are increasingly citizens of a media world. Similarly, Coral Hull has a sequence of poems about a kangaroo meat processing plant and while Hull's poem gives an explicit account of what happens in the plant, she also places the whole scene in its wider social and economic setting. Another way of saying the same thing is to observe that what makes Sean O'Brien's poems about mid-century, post-war, consensus England so powerful, is that he loads them with precisely notated cultural, historical and social details; things like *Penguin New Writing* , steam railways, demob suits etc...This is why, for example, Peter Forbes gets it so wrong in his article 'Why the New Popular Poetry Makes More Sense', when he holds up John Fuller's *Her Morning Dreams* as an example of what contemporary poetry should be doing and says that 'This is the sort of poetry that becomes part of your emergency emotional repair kit.' It's significant that in his next sentence he mentions Auden's 'Funeral Blues'. I think that what this shows is that the dominant model of poetry is still one that says it should deal with universal truths and that therefore poets don't need to attend to the age in which they live. It's ludicrous to imagine at this point in history that poets can go on writing about what Craig Raine once called the 'great, safe themes'.

I think there's also a particularly English dimension to the ludicrousness of writing about universals in a world of accelerated change. There's a scene in Lawrence's *Women In Love* where, just before they go abroad, Ursula and Birkin visit a street market and buy an old chair. Birkin looks at the chair and says 'When I see that clear, beautiful chair and I think of England – it had living thoughts to unfold even then. And now, we can only fish among the rubbish-heaps for the remnants of their old expression.' The answer, he says, is 'to live in the chinks'. Now, for me, this chimes with what the post-colonial critic Homi Bhabha says in his book *The Location of Culture*, that increasingly culture is made out of bits of other cultures, or in the gaps between other cultures. Of course, I understand why a lot of people find ideas like Bhabha's tremendously threatening. I find this tremendously liberating and I'm disappointed to read work without this awareness. And poetry has been at the edge of larger cultural discourses for the past fifty years at least, so it's time we all 'got with the program'!

I'd like to offer a few observations on gender, because it seems to me to be the great unspoken in contemporary British poetry. I'll start with a question: Why do Simon Armitage and Glyn Maxwell attract eager critical and popular attention and yet the work of Charles Boyle is hardly discussed at all? Boyle, after all, in his two most recent collections *The Very Man* and *Paleface*, produces accounts of contemporary urban living that feel just as authentic as anything by the two younger poets.

The answer, I would suggest, is that Boyle doesn't write obviously like a male poet, or should I say a bloke poet. He lacks the hard-boiled voice they both share but, more interestingly, where Armitage and Maxwell ironise male behaviour, Boyle seems to ironise even the possibility of being able to say what male roles are any more. Now, of course, people don't particularly want uncertainty from art, but they definitely don't want uncertainty from male artists. Similarly, it's very rare to find poetry being discussed in gender terms. Most accounts of Tony Harrison seem content to discuss class while ignoring the tremendous internal struggles in his work about masculinity. If his anxieties over 'cissyness' are discussed, then they are usually not related to wider male anxieties in our culture about being involved in cultural production.

If we look at the language Maura Dooley uses in her introduction to the latest women poets anthology *Making For Planet Alice* and the language Jo Shapcott uses in her article about it in the current Bloodaxe catalogue, we find a similar set of assumptions about women poets. The poetry women write displays 'bold linguistic playfulness', 'passionate precision', 'playful intelligence' and an 'erotic and finely-tuned sensitivity'. What all my examples show is the same unspoken assumption: that there is some sort of inherent poetic value in masculinity or femininity. The unacceptable truth, for the poetry world that is, is that the most interesting and important women writing poetry at the moment are generally not writing like 'women poets'. I'd argue the same point about the contemporary men poets I value: they're not involved in a willy-waving contest about who can be the most laconic or tough.

The American writer on masculinity Michael Kimmel puts it well when he says: 'When I look in the mirror [...] gender is invisible to me because that is where *I* am privileged.' I think that can be applied to poets. Most poets do not know they have a gender and that's because poets think that this level of discourse is ideological – which it is – and poets get terribly precious about ideology. A recognition of gender by poets and critics would contribute to some intelligent discussion of contemporary poetry and perhaps even some better poems.

In a culture inundated with printed information, what do you see as the responsibilities of the poet?

I'm terribly uneasy with the Heaney idea of 'the redress of poetry', the idea of poetry as some kind of counterweight of truth and of the poet as a kind of keeper of the 'true' value of language. In this conception, the poet has what Ian Gregson calls 'a *privileged* voice that can make definitive statements of a moral, political and aesthetic kind.' To return to Heaney for a moment in the context of Northern Ireland, the poet, according to this conception becomes in the words of Richard Kirkland 'the central figure who can embody, reconcile and represent the oppositions within his own example.' This is basically an updated version of Shelley's 'unacknowledged legislator' and, frankly, I find it incredibly arrogant. It's also untrue to my own experience of creative practice, because what goes along with it is an emphasis on the poet as intuitive, as a kind of myth-maker or myth-interpreter. I get very annoyed with the idea that the imagination can't be analytical, that it can't be excited by the interplay of economic, cultural and political realities. I think it's significant that I've had to quote two critics in support of my point, because it seems to me that poets are just not interested in challenging the models that our culture and society thrust at them – the exact opposite in fact. With my cynical head on, I'd say that it all comes back to economics. It would be interesting to imagine the career and reception of a Heaney who had followed his own models more closely and developed an oeuvre based on the dedication poem in *Wintering Out* , the one that starts 'This morning from a dewy motorway / I saw the new camp for the internees...'

I think that if the poet has any responsibilities at all then they've nothing to do with the model I've been outlining and little to do with his or her position in a wider print culture. I think that one of the responsibilities of the poet is to register our continuing desire for definitive statements and our corresponding awareness of their increasing unlikelihood; and the way our desire for definitive statements is a nostalgia for stability which, in its turn, relates to ideas of order. I think that the poet has a responsibility to be intelligent, to show that he or she is able to think and, as a consequence, to show that poetry is a space of ideas *not* a sketch-book of observations or touching scenes. I also think that the poet has a responsibility to be an expert in language. This might sound obvious, but one of the unique things about poetry is the particular way it creates meaning so poets owe it to themselves and to their readers to do this in as sophisticated a way as possible. The problem is that people start to get precious about this and start talking about poetry as if it's immune from the dominant systems of exchange and value. Perhaps, the poet's responsibility is two-fold: never to forget that his or her subject is always the same one, language itself; and through this to understand what Vernon Shelley calls 'the nature of subjectivity' at the time at which he or she is writing.

Sarah Maguire

Do you think there is anything to the perception that contemporary poetry shows an over-riding interest in 'personal experience' or confessional work?

I think of myself as being a 'lyric poet', working within a centuries-old tradition. Of the three major genres of poetry, narrative (or epic), dramatic and lyric, it is lyric poetry which is overwhelmingly concerned with articulating the experiences of the self. The American critic, Helen Vendler defines lyric poetry as 'the self's concentration of itself into words'; and James Joyce said that it is 'the form wherein the artist presents his image in immediate relation to himself'. So, as far as I'm concerned, the contemporary poetic genre within which I'm working *by definition* is concerned with 'personal experience'.

I would add two caveats to this position. The first, that it is a mistake to assume that there is a direct, unproblematic relationship between the 'I' in the poem (well, my poems) and the 'I' in the world. Although it's true that I've written a lot of poems derived from particular events in my own life, the *form* of poetry alters the presentation of those events in a radical fashion. So, for example, there is no direct correlation between the 'me' in my poems who is an adopted child, and the me you might get to meet. Form is of decisive importance. Lyric poetry, then, is a *fiction*. James William Johnson says that, 'The speaker [in the poem] is a device for making the invisible visible'. Summarising the developments in deconstruction in literary criticism which have argued strenuously against the notion of the speaker in the poem being the poet-in-the-world, Johnson writes that, 'The poet-surrogate is replaced by the figurative voice… that makes the verbal world of the lyric a visible world to the mind of the reader'. 'Personal experience', in other words, is a trope, a literary device employed by lyric poetry.

Second, I would stress that 'personal experience' does not necessarily support an indulgent, individualistic position. What we make of 'personal experience' depends on how we define the self. If we think of ourselves as being atomised individuals living hermetically sealed lives in which 'society' does not exist, we will write Thatcherite poetry – poetry, by the way, which is still open to a political analysis. I think of myself as being an historical subject, so I suppose I try to write poetry which is open to history and politics. Not in a programmatic way – that's called polemical poetry – but within the traditions of the lyric. What I like about the lyric is the way in which it can, through metaphor, juxtapose and hold in suspension all sorts of events, ideas and sensations. Again, form is of overwhelming importance. Writing a newspaper account of a major political event is an entirely different process to writing a poem about (or in relation to) that event. The newspaper report would have to be linear, factual, objective. The poem could throw together all sorts of objects, impressions and feelings.

What important influences have shaped your current interests?

I read an enormous amount of poetry as a child and teenager, working my way through an anthology called The *Albatross Book of Shorter Poems* (I think) and then the *Longer Poems* (I have a distinct memory that Pope's 'The Rape of the Lock' was not quite what I expected, and something of a disappointment too). I liked Dylan Thomas when I was younger – someone I never read now – though I think his musicality and the vividness of his imagery was no bad thing. I also liked Sylvia Plath (of course) because I was an intense adolescent; again, I think (I hope) I absorbed something more useful about the way she handles *things* (Plath is a very *thingy* poet) and the spareness of her later work. I also loved Keats and can remember being very affected by his letters, and I had a great attachment to John Donne, amongst many others.

Then I stopped reading (and writing) poetry in my late teens, partly because I was working as a gardener (and was knackered), partly because I'd become very politically active, especially in the women's movement which, at the time (the mid-70s) was going through its most Stalinist phase. Poetry was written by men. And it was a bourgeois indulgence which, in Auden's crushing phrase, 'made nothing happen'. So, what with separatism and functionalism, I decided to give the whole thing up (well, I tried).

In my mid-twenties I gave up giving up, although not without a struggle. Two poets changed me. The first was Ezra Pound. I found that I *had* to understand how someone who was a fascist could write such compelling lyric poetry. So I set to work reading everything he'd written, and everything I could find written about him. I still think that his work – especially the Imagist and *Cathay* period poems – and his critical exhortations (in the *ABC of Reading*, the *Blast* manifestos and elsewhere) have had a greater impact on my work than anything else. 'To break the pentameter, that was the first heave': it's Pound's music that's so important, that and the astringency of his language.

The second poet who really got through to me was Tom Paulin. I was standing in an English bookshop in Amsterdam in the middle of having an appalling nervous breakdown in the very early 80s, when I picked up *The Strange Museum* and read 'Before History', the first poem. Not only was I captured by the 'mood' in the poem (waking up early and alone with rain 'falling through the darkness' – I have an almost uncritical love for poems with rain in them), but also by the fact that Paulin was talking about *History*, history in a Hegelian and Marxist sense. I was over the moon. To understand my elation you have to know that I was brought up on this stuff: I'd joined a Gramsci reading group at the age of nineteen, for God's sake, and had become delirious with joy (I mean this) the first time I began to grasp Marx's theory of alienation in the *Early Writings*; even now, it's true to say that few things turn me on more than a good wodge of critical theory. So, to find Paulin who, in *The Idea in History* (yes!), could write: 'When the mind grew formal / Caught in the nets of class / History became carpets, chairs', made me astonishingly happy. Here was someone who wrote sensually rich poetry which was informed by ideas, ideas that I loved. So then I read everything about Paulin and everything he and his contemporaries had written (I'd read Heaney years before that, and Muldoon in the early 70s) and I was off.

The American poet Adrienne Rich has also had a big influence on me, not in terms of the way in which I write but, again, her interest in politics. More recently I've admired the work of Jorie Graham, because of her intellectual ambition, and the architecture, intelligence and sensuality of Mark Doty's poems. Like a lot of my contemporaries, I turn to American poets for inspiration. I find the parochialism and the pat, 'light verse' strain in contemporary poetry written in these islands dispiriting, to put it mildly. I'm hoping to translate some Palestinian poetry sometime soon (I've visited the country twice for the British Council in the last year) so I'm trying to read as much contemporary Arabic poetry as possible, which is hard because it's not been terribly well translated, by and large (Arabic works much better in Romance languages than in English), though anyone who's interested should take a look at *Modern Arabic Poetry* edited by Salma Khadra Jayyusi (NY, Columbia University Press, 1993).

What are your interests regarding questions of sexual politics and gender in poetry?

My interest in sexual politics and gender issues in poetry is overwhelming: definitive, really, as I'm a woman poet. One of the things that preoccupied me when I started writing was, inevitably, why were there so few women poets? Was it simply that we weren't any good at writing poetry? But then why so many women novelists? It took me years to find answers to these questions. Maybe I should briefly summarise some of the conclusions I've reached.

Firstly, women writers had to face almost insuperable difficulties, because writing was hardly a respectable activity. The reason that women dominated the novel (and they did at the beginning) was because it was a new literary form, which was looked down on by literary society (read Pope's *Dunciad* if you have any doubts); also the novel became preoccupied with questions of femininity

– with increasing respectability (rather than literary approval) once Richardson's great landmark *Clarissa* was published in 1747.

Women who wanted to write poetry faced special problems, because an apprenticeship in the Classics was deemed to be essential – and few women were allowed to learn Latin or Greek, which left them with the option of writing the equivalent of 'light verse', very much despised by the elite. However, despite these trials, there were a lot more women poets than we were told about and, gradually, they're finding their way back into the canon (the fourth edition of *The Norton Anthology of Poetry* contains poems by 79 women, out of a total of 355 poets, an increase of 55 women poets since the third edition a decade ago).

For those women who did make it into literary society, or on to its fringes, few have stood the test of time for complex reasons. Many of them were very fashionable in their day – and then have vanished. That's often because they were fashionable for the sake of being fashionable – like performing dogs. The sort of poetry they were encouraged (permitted) to write was often very limited in its scope, and written in a very conventional way. Women poets were rarely ground breakers (*pace* Emily Dickinson – and she was hardly a legend in her own lifetime).

The two great literary upheavals of recent times were Romanticism and Modernism. Neither of them did women poets any favours. Romanticism was probably the most damaging, and its influence persists today. Romanticism had two effects on women – the first of which it shares with Modernism – which (like all revolutions) was to pour scorn on all that had gone before, i.e. (for Romanticism) the highly-wrought, formal eighteenth-century verse, in favour of 'the natural language of men' as Wordsworth put it; and, in the case of Modernism, for Pound *et al*, what they perceived as sloppy and 'feminine' nineteenth-century poetry, arguing instead for a new 'hard, masculine, classical' style. Both movements led to the wholesale rejection of the many women poets who'd done well throughout the century before. The second, more damaging, result of Romanticism, which persisted through Modernism, was for a focus to be forced on the consciousness of the poet – Wordsworth's famous 'I' which dominates *The Prelude* for example. Poetry became synonymous with lyric poetry (as opposed to the epic and dramatic poetry which had formed such an important part of eighteenth-century verse). An enormous contradiction exists between the confidence necessary for a poet to articulate her (or him) self as the *subject* of the poem, and the subject-position which society allocated to women – in effect, a subject-position as an *object* – the work of the woman poet, then is to move from being the object of poetry (all those endless love poems) to being its subject. None of this is easy, however conscious one is of the issues.

As a result of the new wave of feminism which took root in the late 60s, I happen to be living at a moment during which, for the first time in history, it's been acceptable – even positive – to be a woman poet!

What processes lie behind the writing of your poems?
A lot of lying down.

Are you prolific?
No.

How often do you write?
Rarely.

How much editing and rewriting goes into your poems?
Lots.

I seem to write poems in two stages. Stage one is when something comes into my head and I *have* to get it down, there and then, otherwise it vanishes. There appear to be two main provoking factors. One is reading someone else's work that stirs something in me: My poem 'The Hearing Cure' (in *The Invisible Mender*) began when I was reading Jorie Graham's book *Erosion* when I was lying on the sofa, deaf in one ear (this will make some kind of sense if you read my poem). The other is being alone on a long journey, preferably on a train: the first two poems in *The Invisible Mender* – 'Travelling Northward' and 'The Maryland State Penitentiary' – were written as rough notes during the train journey described in the first poem. I hate leaving home, but when I do, I often write – simply because I'm unsettled I suppose; and I love that meditative state trains can induce when they're quiet; just sitting there watching an alien landscape run by is bliss: passivity and rhythm. Other times poems arrive out of circumstance. The poem 'The Invisible Mender' was provoked by the actions it describes, and took two-and-a-half hours to write, from start to finish, something of a record.

Once I've written down the notes for the poem, I leave them alone – to marinate, as it were. And then I go back to them, sometimes years later, and start writing onto the computer, breaking the long prosy lines into small lines and stanzas. Once I've worked out the shape of the poem – the line length, the verse pattern – then I'm off. The rest is tinkering.

The condition I need for writing (stage two) is absolute solitude *at home*. I have no desire whatsoever to go off to some rural paradise (I hate the countryside anyway), because I need my books and I need access to libraries, because often my poems require research. (The 'Travelling Northward' poem, for example, needed a visit to Westminster Public Library to check out the Amtrack schedule for the train I'd taken; 'The Hearing Cure' required research into ears; the many gardening poems I've written demanded I dug out my notes from twenty years ago as an apprentice gardener studying horticulture. These things do not exist in the country.) Although I live on my own, it's often quite difficult for me to organise enough space (days at a time) without work or social calls. Weekends are best because everyone (except me) goes out on Saturday nights; I like to stay in and listen to the World Service. And you thought writing poetry was a glamorous, socially-crammed activity.

I write once in a while when I have no other choice. Deadlines are good. I can go for long periods (two-and-a-half years, twice) without writing a thing, but I don't necessarily feel *blocked* as such, just that there are other things going on. What I won't do is *try* to write. That's fatal, because I write utter crap and that makes me depressed. I could never do those interminable creative writing exercises I force my students to produce at will. Recently, though, I've thought I might like to be commissioned to write – as long as I had lots of time and it was a subject that chimed. I've liked doing translations, because of the way that they exercise your technique (which definitely improves with the years) without demanding you churn up the goods from your own unconscious. Recently, I translated a sequence of poems by Marina Tsvetaeva, *Wires*, which I loved doing – especially because it wasn't my nightmare relationship with Boris Pasternak I had to deal with. So I'd like to do more translating if I can.

cris cheek

What problems, if any, do poets share, regardless of their stylistic allegiances?

I try no to be to prescriptive towards either my own or other writers' practices. Pursuits, undertaken with appropriate energies of engagement, mindful of integrities to each pursuit, frequently produce 'results'. All poets are putting marks together. One beside another, sometimes one on top of another, often in proximity and on the same page. Writing is a registering of communicative consciousness. It is a conversation between what goes out and what comes back. It leaves differing forms of residue – a resonance, a stain that spreads or evaporates. Writing is oral, gestural, aural, spatial, temporal, textual – re-combinations of and interplays between. There is social text and space as text, as much as 'printed' text. Listening and reading, inner and outer voices, are integral to writing – they are in themselves processes of writing. Writing involves 'performance' in its every respect.

Books are made out of other books, writing out of other writing. Even the oral carries the imprint of the book in a literate culture. If I write 'poypt', as an attempt to articulate the opening mouth of a river fish pouting out an only partially consumed mouthful of food, that word 'poypt' is henceforth out – a neologism in potential usage. Of course, it may never be used again. Such are the specific workings of usage in language. On the other hand 'poypt' might become part of common parlance in times to come.

All writers are in these temporal workshops of language. They try to float or stack or buckle or weave parts of language together, in differing orders, to make it do something that engages and resonates with their curiosity and locates it in a world. Writing reveals decision at its every nano-moment, telling specific stories about language. Sometimes this is a 'make-do' to fit into a particular context. Sometimes, even if it doesn't 'do' anything for the writer, it might nevertheless, perversely perhaps, 'do' something for another.

Differences proliferate, between writers who write only 'readable' texts, readers who read only 'writable' texts and variations turn and turn about between these.

Much writing, of necessity, goes undocumented. Nobody notices it or knows about it except the writers (I'm thinking here of a 'remarkable' exchange in a social context, shared by two or more – profound, memorable, hilarious, unsettling and so on – just as much as the writing which has yet to leave the house or 'see the light of day'.) Writing is a process of interactions, a conversation, a form of collaboration within the broad context of language.

For some readers, who like their writers to be Writers and don't want to be Writers themselves, I've already gone too far here. For some Writers who like their readers to be Readers, the idea that readers might be writers is anathema.

There are those who consider themselves and orient themselves in relation to Literature from within its conventionalised parameters, enjoying the comforts of such protection – using the author as a sea wall against the proliferations of fictions in their world (as Foucault would put it) and there are those who orient themselves in relation to Literature with some discomfort at those 'territorialised' boundaries. Strategies for boundary 'maintenance' or boundary 'blur' differ. The ethos underlining such strategies defines significant differences and they can coagulate into factions of friends and allies – even clot into posturing. My own preference, implicit in my definition of what a writer is and does, is for rendering the boundaries of Literature more porous to the world. To morph its edifice, by sustained exposure to detailed aggregates of quotidian curiosity, cultural practices that are less immediately familiar to me and values that challenge me and those cultural values to which I have become acculturated.

What's going on in contemporary poetry that interests you?

— Growth of audiences for poetry and language arts through performance enquiry.

— Orality re-ascendant. Spoken word in performance and on CD and as part of CD Roms and incorporated on sound files into Web Sites.

— Proliferations of dialect writing (and 'nation' language writers such as Barry Masuda in Hawaii), non-standard spellings and cunning neologism.

— Proliferation of regionally dispersed venues for readings / performances, conferences. More of a de-centralised network.

— Readers becoming more encouraged to recognise themselves as writers, by interacting with texts through intensified paratextual and peritextual play and through compositional structures related either directly or indirectly to hypertext – not that they are particularly new. Both the up and the down sides of such developments, in electronic and book formats.

— Typographical experimentation encouraged by computer tools.

— Post-Guttenburgian reintegrations of word and image in the 'new illuminated scrolls' made possible by computer tools.

— Growth in electronic publishing that provokes strategic interventions for distribution and thus for extending audiences and re-invigorating writer / publisher explorations of the book as a site – an environment with an ecology of materials.

— Dispersal of centres of power for publishing. Small presses can spring up almost anywhere now. One of the resources now available to me that encouraged my move out of London is the proliferation of e-mail and the internet. I'm active on various e-discussion lists. I love such a blur between public and private correspondence. 'British-Poets' moderated by Ric Caddel is useful as a forum in which to talk with some peers in the UK. 'Poetics', from the Electronic Poetry Centre at the University of Buffalo, has many writers with whom I feel some affinity subscribed and is a valuable source of addresses and e-dresses for those who are not to be found there. Ht-Lit feeds my curiosity with developments and potential applications in my own practice of hypertext literatures. Lit-Sci for discussion between Literature and Science. The Live Art List, which occasionally announces intriguing internet collaborations. Finally wr-eye-tings is a list I helped to initiate and it focuses on discussion and (thru a scratchpad set up by Luigi Bob Drake of Taproot) some practical exploration of ideas related to visual poetics, sound poetries and performance work.

— mixes of 'live' voices and 'machine' voices through mobile live sampling sound and image production / projection equipment, (software applications developments from STEIM such as 'LiSa' and 'Big Eye').

— ranges of poetic practices rubbing up against each other, sometimes awkwardly, sometimes promiscuously.

What are you reading these days?

Short answer is poetics, graphic novels, essays, newspapers, magazines, blurbs, advertising slogans, new fictions, performance texts, text-based installations, packaging, car number plates (you translate the numbers into letters).

I probably do at least as much reading from a computer screen as from books, papers and so on. The unsatisfactory aspects of the screen in respect of paratextualities and peritextualities frustrates this reading to a certain extent. I do believe that electronic writing and the book will come to have a symbiotic relationship – both have much to offer, both are necessary.

Reading and listening nourishes all of my interests. I'm particularly keen on 'procedures'. Modernist, High Modernist and Post Modernist texts, but also earlier models teach me to challenge my own work.

I pay careful attention to most of those poets in anthologies such as *Conductors of Chaos*, *Out of Everywhere*, *Dub Poetry*, *In the American Tree*, *Anthology of Concrete Poetry* and *Breakthrough Fictioneers* – mindful of the use for such anthologies, but preferring by far to read actual 'bookworks' by such writers.

Equally important might be the question: What am I listening to these days?

The short answer to which is, a range from Varese via Willie Nelson to Bjork, Tricky, Mikey Dred and DJ Spooky via musics from Madagascar (from the south-west especially), Greece (dances from Ipyros and Rembetika), Tanzania (DDC Millimani Park), Pakistani Ghazals, Malian Praise Songs and Mongolian Long Songs. This listening influences my playing sound (particularly on the clarinet) as much as my compositional approaches.

General response to socio-political questions in Section 3

It seems not feasible that any writer, over a given period, doesn't project, in some way or another, their attitudes towards living, their values, through their language constructions; their work. What processes and strategies one uses to put one's writing together speaks volumes about how one experiences and values one's experiences of the world. I would consider myself a non-violent pragmatic anarchist. I'm keen on humane propositions, bearing in mind that mistakes, misunderstandings, doubts and confusions are part and parcel of much everyday life. My interest is to make interventions into that quotidian. I take care to value that which might not appear to have value, that which might be easily edited out, that which reveals contradiction, is awkward or uncomfortable to my liking and the such. Making a pot of tea is as integral to social interaction as ludic philosophical debate.

Dominant social, political, cultural, spiritual values have structured the language we speak and write. They privilege specific vocabulary, they territorialise specific syntactical structures and rhetorical cadences. To ignore gender issues in regards to writing is to deny the facts of the society which is the English conversation. In saying so, issues of the specificities of other languages and of translation from one language to another are raised. From one 'tongue' to another tongue, writing moves.

Do you have any interests in other art forms which cross-over with your poetry? In what ways do you find other art forms informing and influencing poetry?

I find myself gradually re-approaching Literature and Literary practice, after a couple of decades effectively wandering the highways and by-ways of cross-artform and interdisciplinary collaborations. Working as a writer alongside movement-based choreographers, sound composers, video artists, oral historians, photographic documentarians, community artists, reminiscence workers, educationalists, health practitioners, cultural programmers, independent arts producers, critics and designers.

I approach work in any art form simply as work. I am not primarily concerned with whether it is visual art or music or dance and so on. Such categories mean as little to me as I feel they mean to many contemporary practitioners. Work is hopefully trying to do something, to make something happen, to make-do in curious ways, to ask pertinent questions, to challenge tired strategies whatever its disciplinary basis. However, more and more of what for me is the most acute practice, teases discreet boundaries through interdisciplinarity. Hence, Artform category doesn't concern me much.

Across twenty years of working as a writer, I have been closely involved with Sound Composition, Photography, Independent Film and Video, New Dance and Installation Art, both as a practitioner and as an audience.

Venues have ranged from the Laundry on Lambeth Walk to the Royal Albert Hall, radio and television broadcasts.

My interest in movement-based performance and Contact Improvisation (the territories of dance I felt closest affinity with) have perplexed others. Quite simply, I have often found the head-propped-on-the-bar side of poetry circles and poetry events the more odious of its delimiting features, the most mawkishly male and most boringly 'head' orientated, with an aversion to anything from the neck down other than 'straight' sex. Working in 'jgjgjgjgjgjgjgjgjg…(as long as you can say it that's our name)' with PC Fencott and Lawrence Upton, shifting from multi-voice pieces performed with the text held in the hand, through memorised texts, led to a realisation that involuntary gestures integral to vocal projection (not necessarily by any means of the ejaculo-improv persuasion) broke through acculturated physical habit (begging questions of Bourdieu's formulations of 'habitus') to suggest body-mind oralities that still interest me greatly. Consequently, 'voice' remains a strong component of my work, not only in poetry, but in its widest applications and cultural presence.

Do you write with a pen, typewriter, or computer? Does this influence the kind of poetry you write?

Much of the work I've been writing for the past five years has involved variations on the following process – here delineated in its most extensive.

Differing technologies impact on the working process. Oral and textual both contribute to the writing.

Notes are made onto a dictaphone, while walking, driving, in conversation, watching TV, listening to the radio. Notes are also gathered in notebooks, which generally last for a year or so and become strange environments of material accumulation.

Such 'recordings' are transcribed. Often the initial port is a handwritten version into another notebook or onto blank sheets of A4.

Such writings are then 'translated' into Quark XPress on a Mac. At this point, more decisions about page format, font, line breaks and so on are taken. This stage can take several versions. Each page is 'read' as much as an 'image' as a 'word'.

A further stage can occur when the print-outs, in large type, are placed into a grid blue-tacked onto a wall and then that wall of text is the site of the generation of further material. At such a moment the whole process might loop back through being spoken on dictaphone, and so on.

Most of the writing I do these days takes between two to three years to settle into a version that can leave the house. Often several 'versions' will be teased out and deliberately referred to. Each 'poem' becomes its total process and accumulated 'versionings' under a 'family' title. Trying work out at readings and performance can often inform such a protracted editorial process.

Eva Salzman

Apologia

While many writers mainly just try to get on with writing and living, others – critics, reviewers, agent provocateurs – earn their pennies inventing agendas for us. So here we have the literary life.

For example, take the artificial division between the oral and written tradition. Simple words don't warrant performance!? And performance doesn't warrant an accompanying printed volume. Audiences used to follow the written libretto during an opera, and this practise in no way diminished the integrity or importance of the singing.

Many writers elude neat categories; Good Lord, even page poets pay attention to performance. Mumbled words by the artiste hunched over his lectern is passé – though the polarisation described above has led some fine poets dangerously close to vaudeville as they end up nearly sacrificing verse for the spiel. The art of public reading is to be yourself – that is, your best and most entertaining self – but in a more projecting way. As with the ballerina's 32 fouettes in Swan Lake, the virtuoso feat looks easy to execute.

Performance poets often price themselves out of the non-cabaret market with astronomical fees; meanwhile, page poets don't get asked by cabaret venues. Sour grapes? The arrogance I've experienced has mostly come from performance poets whose money-earning capacities have gone to their heads.

I remember one poet shitting on her audience from a great height, because she'd been called last moment as a replacement. The fact that her co-reader was Derek Walcott made her look just mildly ludicrous. I'd recently co-founded an organisation, Brighton Poets and my offer of a £100 reading was rebuffed by this poet. Fortunately. For £100 – an amount most poets couldn't afford to sneeze at – she'd stay at home. I hope she did.

Another performance poet reads and runs, never staying to hear his colleagues; last time, he ran out on Roger McGough, whose own attitude is more flatteringly democratic and embraces even those who apparently don't speak to the people, for the people, but rather for the page (which the people don't read?).

How insulting to reduce poetry audiences to the lowest common denominator: the easy catch-phrase, the trendy subject. But chutzpah, a monumental ego and a strutting-peacock dress-sense does not equal art. (Beware these impostor street-wise types with their fingers on nothing more than their own pulses – and another bit of their anatomy.)

Before I turn this rant on myself, I might mention how the indulgence of it fits neatly with the performance vs. page question. It's very pleasant to expound from my cell. Nobody can tell me I'm wrong, partly because opinions can't be wrong and partly because I can't hear anybody who might disagree. For the writer, there is an advantage in the one-sided argument and a comfortable distance from the audience.

But let's face it. We all want to be read by somebody and need proof that somebody exists. We sense the great void in which our words will disappear after our deaths, but the idea of such a void while we live is unbearable. I know I have two readers anyway – very charming and old-fashioned gentlemen correspondents, one from Hertfordshire and one from Germany. Others *might* buy the books to fit in with a collection, but that doesn't mean they've ever read them. Hell, even the critics don't always read them. So, how does one get appreciation without exposing oneself to the danger of rejection?

The writer in me is both exhibitionist and voyeur. The exhibitionist is thrilled at the idea of public display – an opportunity to be the centre of attention in a perfectly legitimate and justifiable way. But panic soon overtakes the thrill. Performance is a superbly gratifying terror – the fairground ride you only enjoy after it's finished.

It may well be that being a twin has utterly confused any issues I have of 'us' and 'them': whether we're talking about the writer's affair with the reader/audience, the marital strife between writer and critic, relationships, the class system, or the devil's advocate lodged in the writer's self. I could never argue one thing without arguing its opposite. Perhaps I want permission to carry contradictions in both my life and work.

A dance piece I choreographed some years ago ended with an angry exit and the performer's refusal to come back on stage for the applause. I wasn't really renouncing the audience or making a political statement. It was more to do with atoning for the guilty pleasure of making a spectacle of myself. People call me confrontational, but the most difficult confrontations I have are those with the self.

Cant, Rant

The Oxbridge male-dominated literary world is another boring facet of the class system in this country. (Of course my cliché-mongering can be adduced to, if not excused by, my nationality.)

With one of *those* degrees you can write the most awful garbage and someone will no doubt write an (equally incomprehensible) review praising it. One reviewer of my first book spent paragraphs on my 'I's'. I was reminded of my university essays – pure academic indulgence and not meant to be read by anyone other than the person marking it.

Poets can be so rude with their hermetic posturing and critics equally asinine with their pretence at grasping what was never meant to be comprehensible. (Disgracefully prejudiced, I always imagine that writers in love with their own erudition and obscurity must have sexual problems.)

Nevertheless, I see no reason why writers should explain every rivet and archway any more than the architect who simply expects you to live or work in his building. (I happily break every rule I claim to adhere to – I don't write either to be accessible or not, but should anything happen to fall in either extreme, fine.) Poetry may not be practical of course, like architecture, but then neither is religion.

I'm sick of poetry presented as populist art. As a tutor, I'm often obliged to pretend that everyone can do it and do it well. It must be the only activity in the world which anyone can do. I've no problems with snobbery in the face of such nonsense. My heart often sinks at the sight of another bunch of New Poets – which usually means New Women Poets (more of this later) or New *Young* Poets. There's so much poetry around, it's hard to find your way through the wilderness.

Publishers like Bloodaxe, who effected great changes in the presentation of contemporary poetry, began to collect the full set in a shameless, arbitrary way. Eventually, their Christmas cards grew to folio size proportions to accommodate the growing list of names. It was like they were hedging their bets – unsure what was good anymore. Maybe nobody knows but Father Time. Still it doesn't stop the young lads from setting the canon before any of us are dead.

Can't Rant, Will Rant

Is it predictable to talk of British conservatism, an irritating resistance to change and new ideas, an unwillingness to be in the front line?

In large part, newspapers and editors have very little vision on this score, hopping on board a bus which someone else has serviced and paid the petrol for. Stories make stories, as they say. Rarely, have I known editors to risk their reputations with an unknown.

It's not good form to be confrontational or angry, at least not in public. Maybe this sensibility partly accounts for the difficulties women writers have making their way in the literary world; very often, anger is closer to the heart of their creativity and it becomes a matter of pride and loyalty not to deny the very thing which both fuels their art and stalls their careers.

Suddenly the militant feminist rears her (not so unattractive) head, due to the realities of being female in the literary world. The politics of language can never be escaped; the only difference is that the political language of the male is implicit – the very standard – and so rendered unpolitical: female writers' concerns are politicised in a more literal way, whether they like it or not. And I don't. To reduce our work and concerns to political tract is to diminish them considerably.

One More Rant

Since the Ted Hughes volume *Birthday Letters* came out, I've had more media attention than I'd had in a year previously and most of it to do with my liaison with a male poet whose star is dazzlingly in the ascendant. Although I couldn't possibly climb on the anti-Hughes feminist bandwagon, my experience rather confirms the idea that it's easier to get noticed via a man, rather than on one's own merits.

But how could I jump on the anti-Hughes bandwagon? I know all about the complexities of co-habiting ambitious young poets from different cultures. In my case, the literary soap opera starred an American and a Scot. Ours was a household of double poetic vision, double hypochondria and double egos, alternately big as houses or small as worms and so in danger of being squashed.

Who was to do the shopping? The cleaning? The tax returns? Mornings saw my partner propped up in bed with pen and paper. Afternoons saw my partner propped up in bed with pen and paper. Evenings saw my partner...gloriously creative, like student days when I read, wrote, danced, drew, played the piano, while my mother cooked. I've never been too keen on the mundane day-to-day myself and I could only see making such things more palatable by sharing them with another.

No such luck. Domestic molehills became mountains. The ill-humour generated on the occasions I got him into the supermarket spilled over into the rest of the day. Simple things, which might have been made pleasurable – like walking the dog – were out of the question. He hated exercise. Once, my other half strutted around for a day, impressed by the DIY talents he had displayed by hammering into the wall a ready-made spice rack. The joke seems poignant now.

The contractual arrangement the male poet makes with his soul also obliges him to be perfectly useless in a practical way – and proud of it to boot. My haphazard – and equally useless – survey reveals a population of male poets who, mainly, can't swim and can't drive. I risked my life with one newly-licensed poet who artfully removed a streak of paint from the side of a parked car the moment we pulled out. During a chance train meeting with another one on his way home from a visit home (for they like to keep in two), my friend and I separately noticed in his open bag the beautifully folded laundry: his mother's signature.

I drove my partner to gigs, kept deadlines, shared readings. I persuaded *Poetry Review* to showcase him and now they boast about discovering him. But who looks after us women poets?

Creatively, it was an exciting time. A live-in editor is as luxurious as a personal masseur. We were proud of each other. He was fresh from a Scottish council housing estate, working-class credentials in order – his poems, which few had read, scrawled on foxed A4 lined paper. We too fed each other writing exercises: one such poem was written between London and Brighton. I drove.

I began to feel like the rib returned to Adam. A friend wrote from abroad, asking after my partner's burgeoning career. Oh, and could I get him a reading. A visitor I picked up from the station mentioned a talented writer living nearby. Yes, he lived very close indeed, in my bed in fact. I grew surly. I was a writer too. And I could drive.

Calvinist guilt and angst in a Scot is just pure self-indulgent nonsense in an American, who is somehow not automatically entitled to membership of the same Profundity Club. Celts are much sexier than Yanks these days. Could I perhaps get my American-ness surgically removed and the more exotic ancestry enhanced in inverse proportion? Could I go mad? Post-Plath, to be mad, poetic *and* American is just self-indulgent.

My role was organiser, go-getter, the pushy American brimming with energy and ideas (and I wrote). In *Birthday Letters*, I spot references to a misunderstood American vivacity, which a certain kind of academic sensibility might trample the way you would a disgusting insect: not *intentionally* – malice takes an effort one wouldn't want to appear to make – but the squashed creature would elicit little sympathy in retrospect. Plath was undoubtedly ambitious and difficult to live with – always more blameable in a woman – but then probably so was Hughes. Women's shortcomings tend to veer outward, giving the impression that they have more of them.

Before performances, my partner would invariably come down with the flu, if not cancer. I too suffer from hypochondria (tremendously popular among poets). I'd sit there while my partner and another male poet swapped stories (how many kinds of hospital tests have you had in one week – if they show nothing, there's definitely something wrong,) and generally competed as to who was the most impressive sufferer. Hey, I wanted to shout absurdly, *I'm* a hypochondriac too.

I used to despair about such things – and despair about the despair – but where do I get my black humour if not from the fates?

The End

The poetry as rock-'n-roll hype encouraged the cult of the (mainly male) poet personality: i.e. the auto-didact, the Northern, the Celts, the working class heroes, the exotic, the oppressed – but it seemed to be mainly glamorous boys posing on sofas, with shirts unbuttoned.

The image demands you play down your academic roots, watch football and play the maverick. One poet boasts how he doesn't read poetry. Was he a frustrated auto-didact, having been born middle-class and, alas, educated perfectly well? (All these mavericks seemed to have been to the same party; one after the other, the New Generation poets all cite Elizabeth Bishop as a main influence).

And then the real-life meant giving up the real jobs. One married an heiress, another left his job as a probation officer and another switches passions from science (I'm still not clear what avenue of research she'd pursued), to a residency at a prestigious law firm, where she plans to write about 'the emotional realities of those in crisis with the law' – which presumably means those who can't pay their Mishcon de Reya bills.

Have I missed the boat, not 'selling' myself as dancer, choreographer, exercise teacher, out-of-print book searcher, actress, antique dealer, amateur piano-player, waitress, exercise director at an Orthodox Jewish diet centre, not to mention science dabbler? I thought it was rude – and American – to talk too much about yourself. Anyway, I never did such things for publicity – only out of necessity or, more pleasantly, passion.

I refuse to acknowledge (being a twin) the division between one sort of writing and another. Recently, I've read: *Angela's Ashes* by Frank McCourt – who also happened to be my high school English teacher; *Regeneration* by Pat Barker; *The General* (about the Irish criminal mastermind Martin Cahill); *Hidden Lives* by Margaret Forster; *Manhattan Nocturne* (a detective novel) by Colin Harrison; *Bury My Heart at Wounded Knee* by Dee Brown; *The Architect of Desire* by Suzannah Lessard and, finally, *A Suitable Boy* by Vikram Seth (a book I'd been saving up in a rather anal way; reading is one profound pleasure I don't have to feel guilty about). I have no rhyme or reason to my reading list, or life. I still harbour the notion that eventually I'll get round to everything.

Maybe this erratic reading and all my careers come out of a strong sense of the limitation of my life. And this insecurity mitigates against the confidence needed to bluff your way into the literary world.

When I purchase clothing, it's expected I will try on a number of outfits before I make my choice. In different poems, I live out possible scenarios, which doesn't always make it easy to return to the real one. The art of re-invention is necessary for the poet, in her writing and in her life. The idea of arrival is repugnant to me, suggests an unbearable stasis or ennui. Rather, I want to always be in the act of arriving, or to make the same arrival over and over again, until I can get it right.

Chant Rant

Nam Myoho Renge Kyo

Miles Champion

Is it a responsibility of the writer to make their work clear and easily understandable?

The writer's responsibility is toward her writing.

Should poetry be difficult? Does 'popular' necessarily mean 'simple'? Does 'abstract' or 'experimental' really mean 'elitist'?

What does the word 'abstract' mean in this context? De Kooning said that you can't draw the figure and you can't not draw the figure, and this would hold true in terms of how I regard the relation between poetry, language and representation. Similarly, Bob Perelman and many others have argued – correctly, I think – that there is no such thing as non-narrative writing, nothing that a reader will not be able to narrativise. So, although in this context, and given the oppositions you have set up, I know I'm supposed to take 'abstract' as denoting a kind of writing I find engaging, I still feel puzzled as to what an 'abstract' writing might be. Is 'abstract' writing 'difficult' writing? It's hard to think of something being difficult when one is dealing with such everyday things as words. By this I don't mean to suggest that a work such as Peter Seaton's *Apprehension* is without its difficulties, but merely that one can open oneself up to 'difficult' writing, to writing which, in Guattari's terms, makes a minority use of language, in ways which happily obviate the appeal to shared traditions and a conventional, normatized approach to sense or meaning (it's worth stressing here – as Bruce Andrews so often does in his essays – that the concern of such work is rarely the bypassing of meaning, but rather the *risking* of it and the revealing of its constructedness). To be a foreigner in one's own language need not be a distressing experience. (How depressing it is, for example, that there are readers who have had John Ashbery's poetry 'explained' to them by Harold Bloom... in this sense, the poet's impulse must always be ranged against that, or those, of the explainers.) I suppose much depends on the kind of linguistic occasion a reader wants... I certainly find many of the daily poems in *The Independent* more difficult to read than, say, Peter Inman's *Vel*. What *is* difficult, perhaps, is to write a work which truly is difficult, especially when one considers the relative complexity of the structure of that work, against the complexity of the structure(s) outside it (Kit Robinson's 'Beef sources / are more obscure / than any writing').

The word 'abstract' has little use as a literary term for me – it tends to occlude what is really at stake, at work, in a poetry which might mistakenly be described as such. Steve McCaffery's notion of 'diminished reference' is more useful, implying as it does the impossibility of a total banishment of reference (and narrative too) from the domain of language; but then, perhaps, all poetry diminishes reference to a greater or lesser degree. Context and use (Wittgenstein's twin criteria) erode the arbitrariness of the sign, making it very difficult for us as readers to free up even phonemes from their referential dimension(s). This is the structure in which poetry nests, reaffirming and yet problematising the relation between sign and referent, because – as Roman Jakobson has written – our awareness of the identity of this relation has to be accompanied by some consciousness of its inadequacy, if we are to prevent our perception of reality from withering away.

The term 'experimental', for me, delineates a narrower band of literature – some of the writings of Burroughs, say, and Cage and MacLow – works in which a writing unfolds under experimental / processual conditions which are frequently given by the writer. This would tie in with the OuLiPo and its notion of itself as a research laboratory tacked onto the factory of literature, inventing structures that other writers are then free to use (and I use the word *free* here very deliberately).

No, 'popular' doesn't necessarily mean 'simple', and it's not that poetry *should* be difficult (one thinks of the sustained-over-decades richness of Larry Eigner's or Robert Creeley's work), but populist arguments for poetry do seem a little odd given that the populace, by and large, doesn't read it. I prefer a poetry which more accurately reflects (or perhaps that should be *in*flects) my experience of life, and this is often a poetry which has little concern with the literary effect of clarity as that term might most usually be understood, but which remains, nevertheless, clearly articulated. I'm reminded here of an entry in Tom Raworth's 'Notebook' for January 1971: '...or poetry as armchair – only the basic chair, or the one so alien it says 'try me', are interesting. The others just changing the upholstery or covers.'

Does 'abstract' or 'experimental' really mean 'elitist'? Well, I have some difficulty with the idea that all writing has to be for everyone. If one must entertain the notion of elitism, I think it is more usefully regarded as approaching from another direction, disguised as the notion that there is *one* correct way of using language, *one* correct way of telling a story (of writing a poem), an insistence that writing remain forever tethered to speech. A book of 'experimental' poetry is no more elitist than a book about gardening (and both books, perhaps, could be subsumed under the somewhat wider heading of 'non-fiction').

What are you reading these days?

Hannah Weiner's *We Speak Silent,* Rod Smith's *In Memory of My Theories,* Barrett Watten's *Frame,* Giorgio Agamben's *The Coming Community,* Bruce Andrew's *Ex Why Zee* and *Paradise & Method,* Andrew Levy's *Continuous Discontinuous,* Steve Evans & Jennifer Moxley's Impercipient Lecture Series, Joan Brandt's *Geopoetics,* Len Bracken's *Guy Debord – Revolutionary*; Michel Foucault's *The Politics of Truth*; also some new poems in manuscript by Tim Atkins, Caroline Bergvall and Deana Ferguson.

Other recent readings and re-readings would include: Jean Day's *Flat Birds,* Larry Price's *Crude Thinking,* Juliana Spahr's *Response,* Gilles Deleuze & Claire Parnet's *Dialogues,* Walter Benjamin's *Moscow Diary* and *One-Way Street,* Francis Ponge's *Soap,* Georges Bataille's *Guilty,* Wittgenstein's *Remarks on Frazer's Golden Bough,* the journal extracts by Clark Coolidge and Bernadette Mayer in *Code of Signals,* issues of *hole, Arras, Chain,* and the 'Plays' issue of *Hills.*

What influences have have shaped your current interests?

Stephen Davis's *Hammer of the Gods.*

What social / political interests motivate your writing, if any?

One can choose to deny or ignore politics in one's work, but that doesn't place the work outside of politics – the rat of politics always gnaws at the cheese of art, as Robert Smithson wrote.

While I continue to find the (these days rather tired) distinction between writing *about* politics and writing *as* politics a valid one (and similar usefulness in Benjamin's assertion that writing which teaches writers nothing teaches no one), I'm unable to dispel the unease which arises from the feeling that this textual space in which I work, and this space in which the writing I read sits, is not where politics happens. Or, to put it less bluntly, that to work in any area of symbolic production seems necessarily to mean working in a politically diluted way.

I've been thinking through my discomfort on this subject again since reading Steve Evans' *The Dynamics of Literary Change,* especially the section on Adorno and the abstractness of the new [and I trust I'm not taking S.E.'s words too far out of context here]: "Too immediate an expression of protest serves to dismantle the 'époché' – the frame or bracket – that preserves art's critical distance from the world, and it does so without truly compensating for the loss in political terms. The tendentious work, though it seeks the reintegration of art and politics, perhaps even the transcendence of these categories in a new and revolutionary synthesis, ends instead in a neither / nor position: neither art, nor politics." And later: "Action within the aesthetic sphere proceeds by way of a primary renunciation; abandonment of direct efficacy in social terms is the price of aesthetic practice. And yet, formal autonomy must be fed with content that can only be social. Actually it is less a question of form and content, art and society, than of a homology between two social forms – the commodity-form and aesthetic-form, for each of which imprintation with the mark of novelty is an urgent necessity."

Semantic ambiguity and formal disruption play deliberate parts in much of my writing (give the man a cigar!), and it seems no longer sufficient to posit a desired valorization of the reader's role as a political justification for such textual effects or indeterminate content. I *am* concerned with a micropolitics of writing which sits largely at the formal level – a 'politicized form' which is mindful of Barthes' view of straightforward representation as being merely 'embarrassed figuration' – but which is also very much to do with the fact that I have a body which is located in the world and which, as Merleau-Ponty would say, sustains the visible spectacle (concerns I find shared in the works of Jeff Derksen, Caroline Bergvall, Kevin Davies, Karen MacCormack and many others). For myself, as a reader, there is a usefulness I would be reluctant to separate from politics in that poetry which makes me want to live, as opposed to making me want to leave.

To what extent should poets be concerned with the age in which they are living?
To a reasonable extent.

In a culture inundated with printed information, what do you see as the responsibilities of the poet?
I'd like to answer this question with a quote from Andrew Schelling's 'Of Maps, Castelli, Warplanes, & Divers Other Things That Come "Before the War" ' (in *Temblor* 2, quote reprinted in *Acts* 5):

> Words are shifting integers. Syntax coils with equal ease through the heavens and hells. That the newsmedia, multinationals, armed forces, and governments on our planet have learnt this, to virulent effect, leaves writers – whether they acknowledge it or not – as the only viable oppositionary force. Responsible users of language, those who Robert Duncan says have maintained 'the ability to respond', stand as never before 'Before the War'. Words in this Era of Information manifest themselves as monstrously efficient instruments of domination and

deceit. The turf of language is one of the dilating consequence. When the war 'comes home' to brain and larynx, and to the space between all of us, Poetry – *writing* writ large *or* small – becomes a mapping of worlds in which both world and map are inextricably at stake.

In what ways does the work you are working on at the moment reflect your formal interests?

Well, the forms are always *intended*. Recently, I've been working on a piece of prose – it's not often that I get to bang up against the right margin with such regularity and the piece is of interest to me, formally, because of this novelty. But, although I'd like each of my works to look different from the last, and while I endeavour to make them so, I have quite a limited interest in formal experiment. The shape of my writing often follows the shape of my reading, with many poems brought into being through, and then subsequently maintained by, their dialogical relation to the works of others. My interest in form, then, is often shadowed by an interest in appropriation – that is, to what extent can I make a work of my own out of the loving destruction of the works of others? But perhaps this is what writing is anyway, given that language is what (and where) it is; as Clark Coolidge wrote in *Mine: the one that enters the stories*, 'writing is impossible, the words are all there'.

In what ways has your early work changed to address your current interests?

I would answer that my early work hasn't changed, if it weren't for the fact that I haven't written my early work yet – I'm hoping to write it later on.

John Burnside

I want to begin by saying that I think writing – all kinds of writing, not just poetry – is essentially a solitary activity. By 'solitary' I don't mean lonely, or hard, or anything glamorous. I just want to say that the method of writing tends to depend upon having long stretches of solitude, not necessarily to write, as such, but for ideas to percolate through and take recognisable form. This suits me very well, as I like to be alone, and I feel to varying degrees awkward and dislocated when I am in 'social situations' for any length of time. There is, for me, something inauthentic about the social. I have a handful of friends with whom I feel comfortable, but most of the time, I like to be alone. Glenn Gould used to say that there was a certain solitude quotient: for every hour, say, spent in the company of others, one might need two, or eight, or sixteen hours alone. I suppose I have a high solitude quotient. So it follows that, temperamentally, I am not inclined to think in terms of groups or schools of poets – there are occasional passing similarities, (which are often exaggerated by interested parties, to support a thesis or marketing strategy), but what I value in poets I admire – and what I aspire to myself, I suppose – is the individual voice, the specific point of view that enriches the world, and makes it more habitable. This is what I look for in poetry – though I understand that other people look for other things, and I feel the need to respect that.

Mandelstam said, 'No, I was no one's contemporary' – and though he may have been referring to his namesake, Stalin, he was also making a point about his writing. We can find ways of lumping him together with other 'Acmeist' poets, such as Akhmatova, or Gumilev, perhaps even Tsvetaeva, but the spirit of his work is unique, just as those other poets are unique. He also said something along the lines of 'Do not compare: the living are beyond comparison', which is too often forgotten, by readers and critics, (though less so than the poets themselves?). One tends, of course, to see how different, even how wayward, one's own path is. Naturally, I can see points of comparison – i.e. points of agreement – between myself and some other poets working now. There are poets whom I admire, and there are those with whom I feel a kinship, for all kinds of reasons. To cite names would be misleading, however. There are a dozen or more poets writing in these islands whose work I admire, but I do not necessarily feel any common cause with them, or at least, not enough to belong to a grouping of any kind. I think the best artists, in any discipline, have that much of a maverick quality. So – being a maverick myself – I am bound to respect other mavericks. What I respect in other poets – and what I value in my own attitude to poetry – is an openness to different ways of saying. Many people - poets and others - pay lip service to this idea; not all live by it. I think there are groups, cliques, support networks – whatever you choose to call them – in poetry, just as there are in any business. I mistrust this tendency to huddle together, which is as strongly as I want to put it.

Of course, there is also the fact that – in order to find time to write – we often depend on grants, awards, prizes etc…and these are usually dispensed by the social adepts and mixers among us. The selection process is bound to be flawed – for a variety of reasons, some of which, apparently, it is not polite to discuss. Not being a mixer, I have to trust to the integrity of others and, at times, that trust has been disappointed. At such times I would be dishonest if I didn't admit that I wished I 'belonged' more, that I wished I was an insider. Mostly, though, I just get on with the work. 'If I do well I am blessed / whether any bless me or not' – as Marianne Moore puts it.

What are you reading at the moment?

I am reading a good deal of Marianne Moore. This is a luxury I have been saving up for myself for a long time: when I finished my novel, *The Dumb House*, and a new collection of poems, *A Normal Skin*, I made myself this space to re-read Moore as a celebratory present. I am also re-reading Moravia – a very much underrated writer, it seems to me. I go back often to writers who matter to me, especially in times of change, in periods of transit. In fact, it seems I am mostly re-reading at the moment – so this is probably just such a time.

I have to admit that I do not make a huge effort to keep up with everything that is happening in contemporary literature. I read on the recommendation of friends, or because I trust a certain writer. Because I had been astonished by her earlier work, I recently read A.L. Kennedy's latest novel, *Original Bliss*, which I thought quite marvellous. I have been slowly reading and re-reading an American poet, Brigit Pegeen Kelly, because a friend in the US sent me a copy of her book, *Song*, which is wonderful in every sense of the word. I find I enjoy much American poetry, and make new discoveries all the time: I was introduced to David Clewell's work just over a year ago by Martin Mitchell, the editor of *Pivot*, and I have been an admirer of Jorie Graham since I read her first two books, *Hybrids Of Plants And Ghosts*, and *Erosion*. I enjoy American poetry, which seems to me diverse and exciting – so, other than the *TLS* and the *LRB*, I tend to read American magazines.

Do you think that the New Generation Poets promotion was a good thing, or was it simply an exercise in marketing?

I have to admit that I was very naive about the New Gen promotion. I was still working in commercial computing then, so much of my time was spent in the offices of banks and insurance companies, or talking systems with other software providers, and I suppose I thought of the New Gen thing as something of a party, an escape, even. I can't say how much difference it made to me – I had a book coming out then, anyway, so I would probably have done the readings I did as part of that. Like others who were on the list, (and perhaps like many who were not), I assume that I benefited a little from the raised awareness of poetry. I didn't do Radio 1, or *Vogue* magazine, or whatever. I imagine what I do doesn't fit in to that particular mould. Still, I didn't see any problem with it being about marketing. I really dislike this attitude to poetry – somehow it oughtn't to be marketed, because that's cheapening it somehow, but as far as the poet is concerned, s/he needs an audience in order to continue publishing. We all know contemporary poetry does not sell – which is curious, because there are apparently so many people writing poetry themselves. There are only a handful of publishing houses with poetry lists now, and they are only there because a particular editor has chosen to fight a really rather hard corner. So I was glad to see a group of people putting so much effort into marketing poetry – which doesn't get pushed much, generally. I thought the criticism of the idea in itself very unfair, at the time, because the people who started the ball rolling genuinely cared about poetry.

Having said that, I soon realised that part of the media were deciding who were to be the 'leading lights' of that group, which of course meant who they could sell to their readers and viewers: who had a curiosity value, who were easy to consume, or whatever – poetry was to be the new rock and roll, the new stand-up comedy, or whatever – (as long as it was dressed up as something else, and didn't just stand there in its undies, shivering). The most astute – the poets who were most in touch with what was wanted, capitalised on that – and I have no criticism here either. Maybe the actual writing of poetry is a solitary, meditative, relatively 'pure' activity, (certainly for me, it's when I feel the closest to being 'authentic'), but going out and selling it (oneself) is a business like any other. The smart players know how to play the angles. It's the same elsewhere – in the giving of grants and prizes, for example. Not always – which is refreshing – but often. I suppose you could say the New Gen promotion was a party after all, a party to which twenty people were invited, though only four or five of them got to eat the jelly. Yet I gained in other ways. I met some good people and I learned a great deal. And the New Gen, as much as anything, made me look at how I was living, and ask myself what I wanted to do – which was more than just write poetry in my spare time, after long days spent manoeuvring around the jobs-worths in IT departments of big insurance companies. About then I pulled together what I'd sketched out of a novel (*The Dumb House*), and set to work in earnest.

What do you think poetry is capable of?

Poetry is capable of raising the hairs on the back of my neck. It can make me feel there is an order – a highly complex, and in no way reassuring or comforting order – in the world around me, an order which I want to affirm, even though it is perfectly oblivious to me or my interests as a transient individual. It can generate a quite irrational sense of general affirmation in my soul, in much the same way as a song by Schubert, or a motet by Scarlatti. It can do other things too – but this is what I am looking for.

When it comes to the crunch, though, there isn't much point in talking about poetry... a good poem is a mystery, an alternative space in which anything can happen, with its own logic and natural laws. It cannot be described or paraphrased, all you can do is read it and enter the space it creates. Whatever holds for music, in other words, holds for poetry. If you say to me: 'What can you tell me about Dufay's *Ecce Ancilla Domini* Mass?' there wouldn't be much to say. Nothing that would help. You have to listen to the music. Once you have done, you see there is nothing much to say about it.

Do you have any interests in other artforms? Have you collaborated with any artists or writers recently?

I have always been interested in other art forms – especially music, visual art and cinema. In fact, I wanted to be a painter once, and only gave up on the idea when I saw I had no technique whatsoever. I couldn't translate what I saw into images – though I could be accused of being impatient, of expecting results too quickly. I like all kinds of music, from Perotin to John Adams. I particularly like songs. I think of writing (not just poetry, but all kinds of writing) and song as a continuum. I recently was involved in a collaborative project with the painter Callum Innes and Alec Finlay of Morning Star Publishing, from which I learned a great deal, about looking at the world; about its representation; about processes of discovery and revelation, and about trust. Because I enjoyed that project – and the art work which emerged from that collaboration – I intend to take part in more collaborations. I have recently been talking to the printmaker Mary Modeen about one project, and discussion has just begun with the Fife-based painter, John Lowrie, on another idea.

The most significant event in my recent life, (with regard to writing, at least), has been my return to Scotland, and moving to Fife. This feels very much like a homecoming and my work has begun to reflect the language, landscape and culture of the country which is both my natural home (in being my place of birth) and my chosen dwelling place, (because I chose to return here, after years away – voting with my feet, as Robert Crawford would say). This does not mean I am suddenly going to begin writing in Scots, or playing the stage Scotsman.

The exciting thing about Scotland is that it is, in spirit, an independent republic, and it is only a matter of time before that republic is fully realised.

My most recent work, (i.e. the poems I have written since I returned to Scotland) reflects this homecoming. I have just completed a long poem, called 'Ports', about the harbour at Anstruther and its surrounding area, and I am working on a sequence called 'Gude Man's Land', about the Gude Man's Croft, or Land, which is a piece of land, usually about an acre, which farmers would set aside for the Devil's use, so 'he' would not come on their land and damage the crops. I am very interested – always have been – in the persistence of the pagan, or the magical view of the world, which could be seen as a metaphor for the persistence of the intuitive, and also for the need to recognise the violence in nature, the not-in-any-way moral or 'bad' darkness of the natural world, which is expressed in energy and growth as well as decay and destruction. Of course, here I am paraphrasing what ought not to be paraphrased. What I should just say is that every landscape I have ever written about, whether it be Northern California, or the Surrey suburbs, has also been, in part, and of necessity, a Scottish landscape, because that is the landscape I carry with me, always. Or perhaps I should just say that I have rediscovered the place to which I belong, as a writer and as a person, and leave it at that.

Caroline Bergvall

Is it a responsibility of the writer to make their work clear and easily understandable?

What kind of assumptions are being made as to the writer's (and the reader's) cultural role? Clarity/accessibility seem to imply normative pedagogy and the reiteration of shared tradition through the production of writing. To be clear and easily understandable would have to do with responding to habitual modes, refraining from exploring, writing within set bounds of behaviour and thinking. And still there will be misunderstandings. So how clear is clear and why is it even a point in relation to art and writing? Yes, the Greeks, but take one look at their tragedies.

Furthermore, in relation to whom do the criteria clarity/accessibility apply? What kind of reader does this address itself to? Who needs protecting and from what? 'Protect me from what I want' truism by artist Jenny Holzer. Isn't it paradoxical anyway that although the Realists aimed to write up, observe, comment on the social world as accurately and clearly as possible, it would be a misnomer to say that Dickens for instance, is accessible, or even clear.

It isn't the writer's role to reinforce normalisations of language and ideas. Nor is it necessarily, since Modernism, their role to refine existing literary forms. It is the writer's role to redistribute language, verbal as well as non-verbal signs. In doing so, the writer plays with and jolts syntactical framings, vocabularies, concepts, cliches, semantic layers. This leads her to question the various semiotic and semiological strands which enable or disable her writing. And enable or disable her process as a writer.

It is an important aspect of a writer's work that writing hits upon blindspots both personal and socio-cultural. Art and writing have to do with the particularity of angle, ways of looking at things, ways of applying oneself to a reading of the world, making it available to be read and be transformed yet again in the process. This never has to do with clarity, but with involvement.

Barthes has shown how textual pleasure (text as pleasure) is never 'clear' (unilateral?) even where the textual strategies deployed might set themselves out to be. Nor is textual pleasure easy to comprehend or describe. What remains clear from the point of view of reading is that a reader who reads without this risk of pleasure is either a bored reader or a conscientious reader. Clarity *per se* and as moral value doesn't come into it.

One could stretch the point and remind ourselves that etymologically the adjective 'clear' and the substantive 'clarity' are associated with ideas of light. The second definition of the *OED* shows a progression from brightness to glory to clearness. As such 'to be clear' might be more closely associated to ideas of revelation (which is never clear) than to a prescriptive approach to writing or a normative definition of the nature of understanding. Not all writers believe in art as revelation. I, for one, am more concerned with writing as a slow, loose, rapid process of plying and dismembering given structures: radical undressings on a regular Saturday night.

Furthermore, comprehension, ease of understanding imply that writing and the writer should chew what the reader can then digest. This remains an oversimplification of the two inter-related activities and transforms writing/reading into some sort of hierarchical information exchange. Isn't it the case that writing, as poetic practice, contains very little hard information? That what it consists in, first and foremost, is the manipulation of information. And that if it can be assimilated to a sense of expanded knowledge, it remains difficult to measure such knowledge in terms of actual facts.

Take the example of a literary area where the notion of clarity, in terms of accessibility and comprehension has remained high on the agenda: the field of translation. Translation being about the cross-point between two languages rather than two texts (Walter Benjamin), one could ask oneself what kind of writing a translator ought to generate and what the translation should aim to carry over from the original text. Does one, as has often been the case, aim to translate the most immediate 'accessible' aspect of the text, namely its overall meaning, its most 'informative' part, while retaining or adapting a semblance of structure? If so, are we not here dealing with translation less as an activity of writing and more as a quick appropriation, a making-available of digested material. Fast-tracking cultures, languages, texts. This attitude to translation reinforces conventions and silences in the arrival language at the expense of the translated text. At the expense also of the promise of exchange and change which translation could facilitate.

Alternatively one could think of translation, and recent theories and examples point in that direction, as a field which allows for the text in the original language to force up an activity of writing and exchange in the translation language. By which I mean one which almost certainly diffuses and stretches the arrival language. A making strange of language which reveals the 'other' text, the 'foreign' language across the familiarity of the arrival language. Sets up the two languages in conflictual or dialogic relationality.

This more open-ended approach to translation relies on a hands-on, punctual handling of literary material and a knowledge of connotive layers in both languages. Not on the formatting of text through a readability value which remains external to it. It is in this open-endedness that modern writing has found its ground, and the writer their responsibility.

What are you reading these days?

Most present: Zukofsky *A*; Goytisolo *Count Julian*; Deleuze-Parnet *Dialogues*; Stacy Doris *Kildare*; *Sleight Of Foot* (RSE anthology of new texts by Helen Kidd, Miles Champion, Harriet Tarlo, Scott Thurston); R. Graves *The Greek Myths*; Burke-Schor-Whitford (eds) *Engaging with Irigaray: Feminist Philosophy and Modern European Thought*; *Le Monde Diplomatique*; *Flash Art*; *Raddle Moon* 15; *Serie d'ecriture* 7.

What important influences have shaped your current interests?

Sex. Bilingualism. Nicole Brossard *Le Centre Blanc: poèmes 1965-1975* . Monique Wittig *Le Corps Lesbien*. More sex. Trilingualism.

To what extent should poets be concerned with the age in which they are living?

I take it as likely that poets have bills and/or taxes to pay, that they go to the supermarket, to the cinema, to restaurants, to clubs, to pubs, to video stores, to exhibitions, to work, to friends, to bed, have sex, are one way or another aware of their gender, and of their nationality. That they are likely to catch the news in one form or another. That they will at one point or another have considered taking up a mortgage or a bankloan, and setting up emotional and/or professional partnerships. That they might break a leg or end up in hospital or visit close ones in hospital. That they are likely to have used a range of forms of transport and that they are likely to have been to an airport, a bus stop, a train station, a tube station, a petrol station, a public toilet. That they are likely to have stood in queues of varying lengths. That they are likely to know how to use a phone, possibly a mobile, possibly electronic communications. As such they are irremediably implicated in the physical structures and psycho-social functionings of the age they live in. Whether they choose to background or foreground this in their work and, more importantly, the ways they choose to do so, is an inescapable manifestation of their concern with the age in which they live.

What are your interests regarding questions of sexual politics and gender in poetry?

Judith Butler in her now classic *Gender Trouble* makes a claim for thinking of both gender and sexuality not in relation to some sort of essence or Nature but in relation to the constructions and constrictions of representation. 'Genders can be rendered thoroughly incredible'. She shares this post-Beauvoir constructivism and body liberalism with a great number of postmodern critics and practitioners for whom the issue of gender or race, is inevitably accompanied by the question of its construction. It is in this respect relevant that much visual and performance art these last 2 decades has seen a concentration on work which deals with the breakdown of the notion of identity and frequently displays a fascination for the human form under duress or in flux. The digitally treated, erased features of a number of photographers' work. The Chapman Brothers' rather conventional, rather blasé mannequin sculptures with their relocated genitals. Cindy Sherman's perturbing grotesque or gothic gender environments. Orlan's surgical face work. Performance artist Stelarc's implanted third arm. Della Grace's widely self-publicised hormone treatment and her coining of the phrase 'hermaphrodyke'. The interest for life-size wax-dolls in recent sculptural art. And of course cinema: the invasion of cyborg narratives. These outline a persistent, pressing cultural obsession with transformation, metamorphosis as a field through which mythically, artistically, conventions become problematised and gender games can be played out. They outline also a recognition of the artifice of behaviour, an obsession with the synthetic, the prosthetic as a positive decrypting of manners and ways. Technology as a denaturalisation process.

Do these remain formal, structural games? Figures rather than actions? A fashionable, superficial play around gender dichotomy? Or do they ultimately reflect a civilisation in full flux? A profound change in the ways in which the collective social reads the individual and vice versa? Not only a renewal of form and technologies but fundamentally a change of context. Here it is that I find Creeley's much used adage 'form is only ever an extension of content' misleading. Perhaps too complacent, disregards even the closest past. Indeed, the formal experimentations of the Modernists have long since revealed the misogyny which allowed for such explorations in the first place. Pound, Joyce, Williams. 'The radicalness of the poetics is matched by the almost unquestioned conservatism of the gender ideas' (Rachel Blau DuPlessis).

Like visual artists, a number of contemporary poets and writers have used gender and sexuality as leitmotifs for their poetic structuring. Have stretched its locations. Are observing how we work our own content and how it works us into form. Are addressing the conventions and memory tricks which make us each feel we 'belong', we don't 'belong', we are 'this' or 'that'. The figures of representation makes our behaviour stick to allocated markers, pointers in the cultural field but they can also confuse by sheer accumulation. Kathy Acker, Dennis Cooper, Robert Gluck, Juan Goytisolo, Stacy Doris, Lisa Robertson...

The seductive familiar. The repulsive unfamiliar. On a large scale this has to do with the organisation of the individual body (incl. gender, race, disability, sex, disease) in its relation to subjectivity and in its relation to the collective body. Foucault. The filtering of behaviour. The violence of silence. The violence of blindspots. Ethical as well as aesthetic.

All this leads me back to Spivak who writes (I paraphrase): How do I, as writer, speak and read the spaces I occupies and is made to occupy. What occupies (preoccupies) such a space.

The writer's space which Spivak alludes to, in contra-distinction to the more sublimating writer's voice, is dynamic, changing, unsettled and unsettling. Similarly, Kathy Acker's development of a writerly aesthetic which avoids looking for her one voice, the poet's voice ('Writer thought, don't want to be God, have never wanted to be God') and gives us over to the confusion and sharpness of interrupted, discontinuous narrative voices and events. Without continuity I cannot read you blindly, automatically, place you, your gender, your sex, your race, your mannerisms, your history. I have to learn to read 'you' with more than a pinch of salt. Salt as the metaphor corrodes the assumptions and viability of the Same, its necessary Other. What is coming through is the particular, the located as starting-point. Intervention, interruption, activity, reactivity. Threat and bravura. Accumulation. To examine the minefield and fairground of representation. The walking breathing archives of representation. Camp applies and unreads historical models through contemporary modes. As such is mainly pointedly liberational. But a gender spectacular which is part of the denaturalisation processes our contemporariness struggles with. Nature is what we make it.

Is poetry for the page, or are you more interested in the oral tradition / performance? In what ways?

Different forms of writing, of poetry, take place according to specific contexts of writing. This is of paramount importance to me. To write for the page implies not only the development of a wide set of verbal manipulations. It can also (it doesn't always) take into account, and as part of the composition, the manipulation of non-verbal signs such as the space of the page, the typography used, etc. This can quite explicitly lead to constructing a writing which acknowledges (not takes it for given) the page environment as its foremost specific context. This is particularly present in the American poet Johanna Drucker's typographic work, in Hannah Weiner's diarist poetry, the conceptualisations of Susan Howe, of Maggie O'Sullivan all of whom however loosely follow on from Mallarmé's attention to lay-out for generating meaning and the subsequent visual variations set up by Pound, Olson, Appollinaire, e.e.cummings.

Concerns explored in this way will be largely different from the work of a poet who sees their main impetus as situated in the setting up of live situations for writing and for whom the page might function as one additional environment. An environment available for scorings (Bob Cobbing, Alison Knowles, Jackson

MacLow, Steve McCaffery) or to the reformulations of the piece on paper (cris cheek). Here again the divide between live performance and page performance is tenuous. Poets who engage their work in both situations, such as Fiona Templeton, Steve Benson, Ntozake Shange will often devise strategies of writing which are informed by this toing and froing between environments and readers/audiences. As such they include rather than exclude a number of formal modes. Similarly, a poet might decide to explore writing through the making of objects, as the Belgian Surrealist Marcel Broodthaers did. Here again the structural motivation and general outlook of poetry will be carried out according to the specificities of the chosen material, surface, medium.

To maintain a strict dichotomy between page-based and live-based poetry strikes me for this reason as quite erroneous and, perhaps more to the point, as symptomatic of a still wide-spread lack of flexibility in the defining of poetic activity. One which implies a stifled understanding of poetry as a genre which can only sustain itself in either-ors.

It seems more pressing and would have more far-reaching consequences to say that: where you wish to place your work, the way you think that space, informs how you develop it. Hence one would be more concerned with the activity of writing than whether it is prose, poetry, criticism etc.

Have you collaborated with other artists/writers on any work recently? How has this developed your poetry?

I have nearly always paralleled my individual writing practice with cross-artform collaborative work and some of my first commissions were for collaborative projects. This has been highly influential on the manner I have come to tackle a range of writing strategies in my individual investigations. It's also been key in making me see how difficult it is to truly engage in the collaborative process, how difficult it is to allow for one's own preoccupations to be altered in contact with another artist or artform, and how infuriating it can be to have to take into account all the accidents, surprises, tensions, last minute changes which the shared development of work invariably forwards. In addition to which, and probably due to the fact that shared work always seem to put one on the line in highly unexpected ways, the emotional stakes feel frequently much higher than when presenting individual work. For this reason, I'm convinced that collaborations require a particular frame of mind, not only towards one's collaborators but also and importantly towards one's own practice, and that there is a right time and a bad time for them.

My last explicit collaboration so far has been with composer and sound-artist Kaffe Matthews. A short but prolific time. In many ways collaborating with Kaffe didn't so much mean integration, assimilation of twos into the one project as working quite clearly quite openly side by side, sometimes even back to back, around the same idea or site and with our respective media or specialist fields. Reaching points of contact more by way of persistent critiquing and observation of each other's parts in the project than by seeking symmetries, correspondences in our specific approaches. We developed several projects together: an interactive sound-text installation, a live piece for a festival in Huddersfield, which we later redesigned for an event at the Union Chapel in London, a sound-text work for Video Positive '95. The diversity generated felt exciting, edgy as well as playful. From my point of view it helped show up some of the difficulties involved in writing text (esp. narrative text) off the page and on to gallery walls or as part of a wider sound environment while retaining the ambiguities of the written page-based syntax. From the perspective of collaboration I was surprised to realize to what extent our insistence on a gap, a distance between collaborators had in quite unforeseen ways added a positive disconnectedness to the environments the audiences were party to.

My most recently completed piece started out as a text installation entitled *Éclat*, a guided tour of a domestic space commissioned by the Institution of Rot in London in 1996 which I later partly rewrote and completely redesigned for its publication as a book by Sound&Language under the same title. I consider this piece, both its installation and the book, to be in part the result of a string of collaborative moments. Aspects, or moments, of the piece were put together through careful and repeated contact and discussions with the curator Crow and later the publisher cris cheek, both artists in their own right. A visual artist, Sally Tallant, took part in the conceptualisation and setting up of the installation as well as in its documentation and these discussions and activities again informed the many stages of the live piece. Her visual documentation was later used with Simon Josebury, designer for the journal *Performance Research*, when I was commissioned to do a 10 page long text-image variation of *Éclat* for their Artist Pages, a section committed to visual work.

Certain decisions made in the work only came about as a result of these close critical dialogues, the time and thoughts other artists committed to it. If these weren't collaborations in the full sense of the word, they still seemed to me to operate along the lines of what remains for me one important aspect of any collaborative process: the way in which it forces into the compositional process a dynamic, at times problematic, dialogue with others and an open-endedness to form. As a result *Éclat* has taken so many forms that I couldn't today trace up an original, the first, the main text of this project. This is making me more casual towards the finished work and is increasingly affecting my writing processes. Attached and unattached, as precise and committed as possible to every new textual condition.

Concluding remark: What collaborations can do for writers is take us out of the artform's conventionalised isolation and force us to relate to writing as part of a wider network of activity and exchange. Which would be about time.

How do you feel about the pieces once they are published and out in the world?
Twofold.

Primarily interested in the text as activity. Not the finished product. The text in the making, in progress, as it takes place, as it highlights its own mechanics, as it grapples with all sorts of material and issues and found objects, as it asks questions of the poet, of the writer. The wandering structure, the transitional architectures, the airport of writing. The text as airport. Nothing stops here but thousands walk through everyday. The relation set up between writing as a continuous-discontinuous gathering of material and my being actively responding to a collusion of structural, mediatic as much as personal experiences. The pieces start 'out in the world' where I live too.

The writer's relation to the published text. The text as product. I'll start by using the example of film-maker Derek Jarman, whose films provide a complex, playful, highly politicised cut-and paste approach to image-making as on-going process. Of which the film itself and as product is only one aspect. Jarman, the collaborator, the film-maker, the gardener, the activist, the visual artist, the writer, the Aids sufferer, extends the films, is part of the film as project. Both as its iconic figure and in actual fact. Interviews with Jarman are conversational, don't close up his films into subjective intentionality. On the contrary, they provide an added open-ended block to the films, a sense of loose, thoughtful as much as implicated continuity between his films and his living. Through film as process and beyond its product, Jarman implicates the viewer/listener's own awareness of images and stereotypes, how we play them daily, complacently or knowingly.

I would like to presume a similar positioning from the point of view of poetic practice: that poetry is a public activity which involves the poet as one necessary, live segment of the writing. Paradoxically, this frees the poet away from their writing: the poet doesn't relate to their writing as complete, the finished text is only one aspect of writing, the poet is one aspect of the work. Which asks us to think through the link between poetic texts and public voice, between private mechanics and public involvement: how and where does this take place. With what implications and why the separation.

Cage's refusal to set up a distinction between private and public, between process and product diminishes of course the value and importance placed on the one, unalterable published text. It places every aspect of writing: out there: over here: out here: in there: across: around: under: in here: all around.

Michael Donaghy

Does 'abstract' or 'experimental' really mean 'elitist'?

Yes. Not that there's anything especially wrong with that. But look at those sexy words used all too frequently to describe contemporary art and literature, 'experimental' and 'revolutionary'. The first is a metaphor filched from science – experimental art doesn't have a control group, doesn't collate and publish its findings. And 'revolutionary' properly describes a brick thrown at a police cordon, not a poem in *Parataxis*. Among the most cherished illusions of the avant garde is the idea that bourgeois art consoles, pleases and mollifies with received notions of beauty, whereas avant garde art shocks and challenges and doesn't seek to please. I'm always dismayed by this kind of self delusion. The audience for avant garde art is a middle class audience that pays to be shocked, or bored, or insulted, in much the same way that Mistress Wanda's clients pay to be horsewhipped. It's an audience that knows what it wants and is comfortable with its rituals and cliches. Whether it's a urinal on a pedestal in 1910 or a poem composed entirely of semi-colons in 1997 ('everything changes but the avant garde', said Auden), the audience expects to retreat from a direct and complex experience of the craftsmanship, to ideas about art.

The most common of these ideas can be phrased as 'Justify your instinctive reaction that this is not a work of art.' In other words, the burden of proof is placed with the audience, where in former ages it belonged to the artist. Whatever the quality of your work, if it strikes the critical powers-that-be as 'anti-poetic', it is *de-facto* worth talking about. Fine. I enjoy avant garde work from Duchamp to Damien Hirst, to poets like Clark Coolidge, but let's not delude ourselves with the naive and sentimental notion that such art is 'progressive'. I'm angry about that pretence. Capitalism long ago defeated the avant garde by accepting it as another style. Yet artists continue to present themselves as an offence to the establishment even as they accept fat cheques from the Saatchi Gallery or attend academic conferences on 'oppositional' poetries.

I feel very strongly that we have to be vigilant about naked emperors, otherwise mediocrities become cultural referents. Any random shape, crash of noise, or verbal incomprehensibility can become comfortingly familiar – the perfect representation of itself – by answering its own echo or after-image in our unconscious. Say your dog pees on the carpet. Everyday we see the stain and eventually we get used to it. Put that stain on a wall, track lit, in a gallery, run a debate on its merits in the Sunday supplements, refer to it archly in advertising – sooner or later it will become iconic. It will have cultural importance, because we all recognise it. It becomes a cultural referent and will provide all those bourgeois satisfactions that the avant garde profess to despise. And all because no one stood up and said it was piss.

Is there any validity in the terms that are used to divide poetry up into 'schools', or are they just marketing devices?

Marketing devices. Either that, or terms used by academics to group poets into convenient geographical or historical chapter headings. Harriet Monroe of *Poetry* (Chicago) cautioned a reluctant Louis Zukovsky that he couldn't just collect good poems for an issue he was guest editing. 'You must have a movement. Give it a name,' she said – and Objectivism was born. Zukovsky was referred to Monroe by Pound who was, of course, the P.T.Barnum of his movement. I wonder how any serious poet can limit him or herself by declaring allegiance to a particular way of writing poetry. As Malcolm Bradbury said in *Eating People Is Wrong*: Sorry, no movement. All made up by the Literary Editor of the *Spectator*.

In what sense are poets working in the 'mainstream' and in the 'modernist experimental' traditions dealing with the same problems?

Aren't these terms a little too neat? Is John Ashbery mainstream? Paul Muldoon? Jorie Graham? They're all 'difficult' poets and they're all highly celebrated and be-medalled. 'Mainstream', like 'middlebrow', is more often than not a dismissive term used by avant garde artists to describe more famous rivals. If 'mainstream' means 'accepted', then Language poetry, for example, is in the vanguard of the mainstream. It purports to challenge the means of production, but when the academic establishment turns its hungry eye on contemporary verse, it turns to the Language poets. In American Universities they are discussed in seminars and anthologised by major publishers like Norton (their books produced in the same paper mills and factory as any other book.) Of course, their poems would never be read by the men and women who work in those factories. Language poetry makes nothing happen.

Where is poetry heading? Is poetry that homogeneous an activity?

Substitute the word 'music' for 'poetry' in those two questions and you see the kind of assumptions made about poetry. Blues musicians on the south side of Chicago, jazz pianists in London, fiddlers in West Clare, Electro-acoustic composers in Rotterdam – we wouldn't dream of measuring them by the same standard, ranking them, or telling them where we think 'music' is going. Poetry is *not* a homogeneous activity. And art *has no direction*. This is spatial illusion generated by early twentieth century ideas about 'advancement' and 'progress'. If it's hard to see this now, it's because the illusion is augmented by the demands of consumerism. Our economy depends on the notion that things and ideas become obsolete and have to be replaced. Products of art and literature can be sold more effectively if they're marketed as 'new' so that newness acquires an all-pervasive fetish value. There was a lot of fuss made about the New Generation Poets, (a public relations exercise in which, to my shame, I participated). But very little of that fuss concerned the exclusion of poets over 40. We're on our guard against racism and sexism, but ageism is built into our economy.

Is poetry for the page, or are you more interested in the oral tradition / performance?
I'm *exclusively* interested in a poetry that takes its direction and rhythm – like all traditional poetry – from the voice. Concrete poetry doesn't interest me in the least. Most 'experiments' with typographical arrangements strike me as silly. I've done innumerable readings in the past decade and I regard the aural performance of poetry an art form. I'm not a performance poet, but I've worked with performance poets and I respect some as poets and many as entertainers, but for me a rewarding poem has layers and requires of its reader maximum concentration and focus. If such a poem goes over well in performance – that's a bonus.

Charles Olson, that virtuoso of the typewriter, said that verse in rhyme, metre and stanzas was 'verse which print bred'. Olson was a fool. Memorizable form evolved according to the demands of the voice.

Are content and form working as one in your poetry, or do you see it working along different lines from such a traditional division?
I'm not sure there is a clear-cut 'traditional' division. Let me explain: on the simplest level, *form* functions for any poet as a kind of *scaffold* from which the poem can be constructed. Stravinsky maintained that only in art could one be freed by the imposition of more rules, perhaps because these rules limit the field of possibilities and escort us rapidly beyond the selection of tools and media to laying the first stone of the work itself. For the reader, on the other hand, the shared language of the poem functions as a *map* through the terrain of a new idea. Traditionally, narratives or arguments are parted into, for example, episodes in which three wishes are granted, or rhetorical points explored. Expressions like 'on the other hand...' warn the listener to bracket the ensuing information and prepare for its antithesis '...and on the other...' exploiting reader or audience expectation.

But I'm more interested in the unconscious or subliminal effects of reading and writing in form. The effect of form on the reader is like the hypnotist's dangling fob watch, familiar from end-of-the-pier shows and B movies ('Your eyes are getting heavy'). We are hypnotised or spellbound by form, because the traditional aural techniques of verse, the mnemonics of rhyme, metre and rhetorical schemes, are designed to fix the poem in the memory, to burn it in deeper than prose. But think of the unconscious effect of form on the poets themselves. This is the most interesting aspect of traditional technique, and it represents the intervention of that presence – or sense of presence – poets used to call The Muse. Any degree of difficulty in a form requires of the poet that s/he negotiate with the medium, and compromise what s/he originally 'spontaneously' intended to say. (So far so good, since one's spontaneous reaction is always more likely to be full of self deception, prejudice and cliche.) That peculiar sensation, that the best image or line simply 'came to us', as if delivered by an unseen presence, comes from our own unconscious of course. The feeling of 'otherness' is explained by the fact that our self-perception is firmly rooted in our waking consciousness.

John Ashbery has used a mechanical metaphor to describe this effect. 'The really bizarre requirements of a sestina,' he told *New York Quarterly*, 'I use as a probing tool, rather than as a form in the traditional sense… rather like riding downhill on a bicycle and having the pedals push your feet. I wanted my feet pushed into places they wouldn't normally have taken.' But surely this is precisely the function of 'form in the traditional sense' – that serendipity provided by negotiation with a resistant medium.

Have you collaborated with other writers or artists on any work recently? How has this developed your poetry?

I've made a poem / film with Miranda Pennell, *Habit*. The collaboration came out of my interest in the formal techniques of the cinema, the way our visual vocabulary exploded in a few decades to include focus pulls, slow pans, montage and cross-cuts, and the way this influenced the other arts. In fact, this proved to be a problem in making the film – 20th Century poetry is so concrete, so image heavy, that it's often a poor relation of film. I realised my task was to undercut or augment the images on screen with verbal rhythms. I also realised I could be abstract, because the film was providing the imagery. I've also collaborated with the *musique concrete* composer John Wall on a poem for voices using sampling techniques – this is more in the order of a piece of music using samples of speaking voices.

What are you reading at the moment?
John Reed's *Insurgent Mexico*. In poetry, I'm struggling to read Lorca in Spanish and I'm looking forward to reading Don Paterson's new collection.

Sheila E. Murphy

Is there any validity in terms that are used to divide poetry into 'schools' or are they just marketing devices?

The concept of 'schools' is very interesting. First of all, such classifications appear to function as a kind of shorthand for readers who don't wish to go into depth when approaching poetry. It's so much easier to call 'so-and-so' a 'such-and-such' poet than it is to read or hear his or her work. But that ease is quite deceptive, because any work worth existing possesses subtle nuances and fascinating flavours that necessarily distinguish it from all other work.

Schools are generally fabricated entities riddled with inaccuracies. For all their fabrication, schools seem to provide structure and create entities that make sense in a kind of literary marketplace.

And although most writers I'm aware of resist the concept of schools as unduly limiting and certainly inconclusive, having a group of individuals with whom one can communicate and think aloud can be helpful and rewarding. One of the unusual aspects of the very word 'school' is that it suggests an organized system of rules mutually enforced by a group of people who are *de facto* members of that school. In reality, such rules have been inferred from practice, which is inherently *a priori*.

I see the function of schools as primarily a marketing function. This calls to mind a relevant phenomenon in the stock (share) market, that of market making. An individual or a group of investors heavily promotes shares of a new or emerging company, perhaps even buying shares and then selling those shares at what may become an inflated market price (based upon hype and manufactured optimism and opportunism).

If anything, most contemporary poetry that functions in an innovative realm (creates or performs something new and / or in a new way) is seriously undermarketed. In contrast, the L=A=N=G=U=A=G=E movement (though I recognize 'movement' to be an objectionable word) was very effectively marketed, even though the lion's share of funding here in the United States continues to go to academics who produce fairly predictable if well crafted work that is primarily narrative and / or descriptive in character and falls in line with traditional definitions of what constitutes a poem. L=A=N=G=U=A=G=E continues to contribute in a highly positive way to the creation of excellent work and excellent critical thinking about poetry and writing in general. This effort shifted the agenda and called attention both to itself and to the issues that poets associated with the movement introduced.

Schools primarily help classify, either accurately or inaccurately. Does classification help or hinder? Maybe both. In any case, classification represents a useful limitation that distinguishes between this and everything else.

What chances and risks are taken in your own work / work that interests you?

Let me begin by talking about work that interests me, which may indeed include my own. Always attempting not to be prescriptive, I do look at certain aspects of work as sources of interest and excitement. I must emphasize that work that does absolutely none of the things I am about to mention has the potential to enthral me. But in general, these are some of the components that light fires for me:

Surprise. On the spectrum of expectation and surprise, work that interests me tends to fall toward surprise. This is a matter of personal taste, and of course it is the skilful integration of these two factors (expectation and surprise) that makes for the most profound excitement and interest. In work as various as that of Bruce Andrews, bp nichol, Susan Howe, or Dennis Phillips, there is the power of opening the range of what is possible. This may occur through any or all the the components that follow.

Vocabulary. The actual word choice or occurrence makes a big difference to me. This flavours poetry or any other writing. I want to hear something in a new way; I want to see new words or familiar words used differently, perhaps with a shift in syntax. I want to hear syllables differently. I want to learn, stretch, be challenged. John Mingay and Carla Harryman present very different examples of this type of interest.

Variance. Truly interesting work needs to demonstrate and embody variance at its most potent. This might entail the shaping of stanzas, use of word repetition, fusion of visual art into text or the reverse, inclusion of music, establishing a pattern and then varying a theme. The work of John Mingay and Miles Champion come to mind as strong examples.

Inception. That which appeared to motivate the work and the form of its inception interest me. It's an aspect of writing that I'm always curious about, and one that can be examined in terms of the range of the commonplace (an area of major opportunity) and the extraordinary. Rupert Loydell's writing and painting alike seem to harken back to what has motivated their very existence.

Flow. In rare works, it becomes clear that the work has left the writer altogether and has assumed a life of its own. This represents an exciting possibility. Work by John Ashbery and John Taggart comes to mind. A propelling insistence that follows an engagement with an area of the (figurative) Etch-a-Sketch or a chantlike quality that adopts participative voice can provide the impetus for this quality in writing.

Why is it that poetry still seems not to fare so well with arts funding / audience numbers and the book buying public?

When considering this question, it seems important to emphasize several specific issues: (1) Poetry's access to the mainstream marketplace; (2) Derivative attention, whereby the public becomes interested in a poet and / or poetry due to a reference to it within popular film; (3) The superstar phenomenon, whereby the public is encouraged, it would seem, to recognize a limited number of names, frequently based upon something other than poetry.

(1) Poetry's Access to the Mainstream Marketplace

Much of the most interesting poetry being written today emerges from independent presses. In the United States, these presses not only lack access to the mainstream outlets for books, that is, chain bookstores, but I have recently been advised that one of the largest of these chains has just instituted a policy that prohibits booksellers from including the work of independent presses on their shelves.

While it is clear why such a thing might happen, the action being taken feels discriminatory and monopolistic in character. Chain stores have an established / desirable (short) shelf life for their books. Revenues might be measured, for example, on a 'sales per inch of shelf space' basis. Whatever lingers in the store for any lengthy period of time obviously has very little prestige and must feel like some albatross the store owner would love to have carted away. After all, the bookstore is there to make money, not to provide a public service. The problem isn't simply a matter of shelf space either. With as little promotion as there is of poetry books, how probable does it seem likely that the book-buying public would march in in droves and buy up book after book of poetry?

The key point is that a variety of alternative systems have been devised for getting out books of poetry, all of them relinquishing the possibility of the mainstream's system. There is mail order, word of mouth, the Internet, but I would prefer to have at least the option of working within the system, where there is a higher likelihood, at least at present, of gaining public attention.

All too often, I meet people who, on learning that I'm a poet, ask: 'Where can I buy your books?' Wouldn't it be nice for me to be able to say 'At any local bookstore.' Instead, my answer needs to be somewhat obscure. I have to tell them that they must go to an out-of-their way independent bookstore (In other words, I have to make excuses; it is as though I'm saying, 'Well, this book isn't a real book; it's something you need to look for off the beaten path; real books are in the real bookstore, but what I've written isn't that'). Even as I answer, I'm keenly aware that the small bookstore may indeed be 'out of' my book or books, in addition to being on its way out of existence.

(2) Derivative Attention

The film *Four Weddings and a Funeral* boosted the sales of Auden's poetry to an amazing degree. Work that had been present and very available suddenly became sought after in a manner unimagined by many poetry publishers, I am sure. It would seem that the film introduced what took on the form of a precious commodity that people wanted to possess, and then did possess.

In the kindred dimension of fiction, we've seen a strong revitalization of interest in Jane Austen's work, due to its recreation on film and on television. This entire phenomenon suggests to me several things: (1) The public might become increasingly and certainly continually receptive to some of the excellent works of literature in the presence of an adequate introduction to them; (2) At present, the selection process that determines which among numerous possible choices is given the nod to see the light of day is firmly in the hands of the producers and publishers with substantial monetary and resultant power; (3) What is ignored will easily slip into obscurity, especially in an age replete with information.

(3) The Superstar Syndrome

Although poetry is a very non-neutral word (We use 'poetry' or 'poetic' to indicate a complimentary view of someone's speech, writing, or creation), the actual fact of a poetry book or performance of poetry receives skewed attention by the press. Two phenomena are worth noting: (1) There seems to be a cap on the number of poets who can be known; and (2) We tend to hear about poets on the basis of something other than their poetry.

To the first point, the superstar syndrome, which I submit is closely related to the aforementioned issue of marketing, is alive and well in all of the arts. The majority of painters starve, while a few make millions. Many full-length films are never released at all, unless as videos. Some very high quality work is never experienced, because it does not fit the marketing model of an 'easy, quick, marketable sell.'

In poetry, the issue is heightened in that very few poets make any money at all on their poetry. Those who do earn the occasional cheque have generally earned a conventional nod such as an appearance at a presidential inauguration. Then it is only upon such superstar status that an individual gains the right to call himself /herself a poet or an artist.

Examples of the second point abound. One of these, the poetry of Carolyn Forché in the US, became known on the basis of her subject matter. Her book, *The Country Between Us*, explores some political realities of El Salvador. The book has sold extremely well, I believe for this reason. While admirable poetic work, the book appeared to require this boost from its subject matter to receive the attention it deserved.

Have you collaborated with other artists / writers on any work recently? How has this developed your poetry?

Collaboration represents an important extension of my individually-generated work. Even as I say individually generated, I'm keenly aware that every creative gesture emerges from a broad complex of inter-related sources, spark points, derivations. That said, I believe that the active commitment to working with another mind introduces a new type of creation, one characterized by boundaries that inevitably seem to spawn new moments, new takes on already existing moments, and different shapes of perception.

Currently, I'm engaged in writing a long, sectioned, open-ended collaborative poem with the poet Peter Ganick (author of numerous books of poetry, including *No Soap Radio* and publisher of Potes & Poets Press in Elmwood, CT, USA). We're creating this work via e-mail, which allows for a fresh interplay and immediacy of response. I'm discovering that I write differently when working in this vein. The sounds reflect the context in which they are shaped and spoken. It is clear to me that the writing I do in the poem with Peter is unique among examples of my work.

I believe that collaboration does a great deal to enhance one's fluency and responsiveness to generative forces of creation. In addition, successful collaboration activates a capacity to flow in a different way from that which one may have found before. At the very least, collaboration activates a sense of enjoyment that enriches the pleasurable feeling one gains from making anything.

One of the most dramatic discoveries that has come to me by way of collaboration is the evolution of a new persona, and with it, a new perspective. That new perspective is formed in part by virtue of a magnetic energy that occurs from the interplay of two minds. Almost unthinkingly, I find myself writing toward, if not to, the partnering writer. There's a unique bond that seems to form from the act of generating or discovering work together. There's also an amazement at what has come, which usually involves work that differs from what one would make alone. Collaboration prods one's energy level, even on a quiet day in the department of making. A form of liberation helps section the mind into a new category of generation.

I might add that the people most likely to engage in collaborative ventures are those who are themselves prolific. Ironically enough, the act of collaboration possesses so much heuristic value that it seems to generate even more action in perception and the making of work. Thus, people who already write a good deal may find themselves writing even more.

Do you write with a pen, typewriter, or a computer? Does this influence the kind of poetry you write?

I write particular poems using particular instrumentation, and I rotate my instrumentation in an intuitive rather than in a methodical way. Some poems need to be made with pens; others are right for the computer. Some do well by being started slowly by hand and then being speeded up during the editing process on the keyboard. I sense the importance of psychometry as well, the principle that our energy resides on objects we have touched. After a reasonably brief period of use, my pens and keyboard echo back to me my energy and my inclinations.

There seems to me a sacredness about the instrumentation of writing. I cherish even the cheapest of pens (tend to prefer them over pencils, although I've found a little place for them in my practice!). I've also been gifted with some quite expensive pens I can't imagine anyone really affording. And the computer is really a wonder. I've used one since late in 1982. Now I have the pleasure of writing on a desktop Acer that is simply tops, along with a wonderful IBM Think Pad 360.

I reserve the right to select from any tools that I think might be right for the type of impulse that may find me at a given moment. The typewriter, alas, is no longer part of this household. My late father had given me a reconditioned one (a Smith-Corona manual upright if I have my brand name right) during high school, when I was about 15 or 16 years old. At that time, Dad had urged me to take typing, so that I would be facile on the keyboard. (He was a speedster in his own typing and probably could have won contests.) In Sister Rosebia's class at St. Mary's Academy, I went through the perfunctory 'f-f-f-space; g-g-g-space' and came through with the ability to think with my fingers. I must admit that I shudder to think of any headlong movement away from the keyboard, as voice-generated poems are not the same for me at all. I once took a dictaphone on the road when traveling on business through Arizona. During that trip I spoke poems while driving (I remember reading that Allen Ginsberg had perfected the art of writing on a pad of paper while driving one-handed). I later transcribed the poems, which were all right, but somehow seemed forced to me, not nearly so fluid.

When the typewriter was the only machine available, I used to rewrite whole poems when I had any changes at all to make in them. This was an interesting experience, in that it transferred my thought capability to my hands, and fostered a sort of grace in the revision process. Now, on the computer, I work much more quickly and feel at liberty to change passages with very little fuss.

Tim Allen

Does 'abstract' or 'experimental' really mean elitist?

No, of course not, but – and it's a big 'but' – the practices of the so-called abstract or experimental poets lays itself open to the accusation of elitism because of the circumstances in which they have to operate. Also, to a worrying degree, a level of operational elitism within certain quarters of the experimental could be said to perversely mirror the image projected by its detractors. I could argue with your terms 'abstract' and 'experimental', though I take it as read that anyone reading this knows what poetries the question implies.

The backdrop to the peculiar position of the linguistically innovative poetries in the UK, is 20th Century poetry across much of the world. Most is related to movements from the 1870s on – a complex history from early Symbolism to post-L=anguage – roots long, convoluted and genuine. Their position is peculiar however, not so much because of the type/s of poetry, but because of the nature of the literary/cultural scene. The relationship of poetry written in English on this side of the Atlantic to what was happening in other parts of the world has always been a difficult one. Literary modernism came to these shores mainly through right-wing American poets who had assimilated Continental Symbolism and Oriental Imagism etc. Their influence was small, and in the 30s even that influence was nullified by work possessing a closer fit with the national taste. The neo-Romantic rump got a higher profile in the War years, but stood no chance against the post-war explosion of 'Englishness' in the form of the Movement. This is important, because it illustrates the contrast between that poverty of overseas modernist influence with what happened in the 60s, the aftermath/s of which lead to this elitism question. Other countries might have their own chauvinisms regarding literature, but the UK mainstream has an anti-modernist stance that is stronger (or more successful) than any in Europe.

However limited the previous foreign influences, in the 60s there was a rich influx of 20th Century poetry from Europe and America in cheap paperback. The Movement might have closed the door on any native innovative legacy, but this deluge of US and translated material was coming in the windows. These poetries were not homogeneous, they were 'various', even at that early point, yet they were all part of the international modernism that the Movement detested. Because they were various (and because the orientation of those who picked up on them was various), they developed in the new soil in different ways. While on the street and the student common-rooms the accessible performance-friendly material (e.g. the Beats) found a ready audience, what had transpired in earlier radical poetics (via Pound/Williams, the Objectivists and Black Mountain) began to find an audience with certain of their lecturers. This was not particularly evident at the time, but it went deep. It was the germ of the populist *vs* elitist polarity, an interpretation of reality more perceived (the result of propaganda) than actual. That doesn't stop it plaguing us though. The results were far-reaching, this melange of cultural input and hybrid had such an influence that a fault line opened up in English poetry that had previously been covered with meadow.

I don't think anyone could seriously argue with this picture – IT HAPPENED. The arguments begin when we unravel values. It seems almost inconceivable that such an exciting influx of influences could be considered negative, but that is exactly what the *behaviour* of the mainstream says, even when its *statements* don't. The way the more reactionary and defensive champions of the native poetries (in their own variousness it must be said), responded tactically to the new influences, was by being alternately aggressive, accommodating, disdainful and, most successful of all, silent. Strategy was never a problem as it was dictated by the superstructure provided by the higher ed. system / publishing-distribution power bases / general resistance of the English to non-empirical thought / low-profile given poetry (particularly as an artform as opposed to a heritage grading tool). The innovative poets said 'OK, we'll mind our own business, we'll go and do our own thing' – which they did. The accusation of elitism, from those who had told them to get lost, soon followed. Again, this perfectly normal attitude, wanting to get on with the poetry and not spend your life moaning about the mechanics of being ignored, has also been labelled as 'elitist'. I get angry about this, because it is an incredible situation. The poetic apartheid that results is both entrenched and unspoken of – a deadly combination.

There are other things that could be said concerning the perceived elitism of the experimentals – particularly things to do with poetry as an artform. Elitism in other arts is fairly nominal, mainly because of money. Plastic art, for example, however elitist in common terms, is given a price tag which dissolves any perceived elitism, because if it is tagged £1 then it obviously is not elitist and if it is tagged £1000 then its worth is validated. This is a game that most poetry, experimental or not, is excluded from.

Where do you think poetry is heading? Is poetry that homogeneous an activity?
No, poetry is not a homogeneous activity. It's like saying painting is – nonsense. What happens however is that certain people behave as though it is and others behave as though they think it should be. The latter at least have a certain honesty about them – their motives are transparent. The real bother

comes from the former, who judge all current poetries on the parameters of the model they favour, an activity so blatantly absurd that one has to ask how they get away with it so effortlessly.

One answer lies in what we call (or more accurately, don't call) schools. The English are not supposed to like 'schools'. Pre-poem, they don't like manifestos or theory; post-poem they don't like analysis or definitions – they prefer individuality, naturalness etc. This is a smoke-screen – they indulge in prescription with relish, but call it other things. Our literary establishment's theories are endemic and we therefore don't have to call them 'theories' – they are called 'How poetry IS'. By pretending that poetry is a homogeneous activity they can put their model forward as *the* good model and not just as good or bad 'mode'. This is the basic modus-operandi of the mainstream. On the continent schools come and go more-or-less openly – a group tending in a certain direction will passionately put the case for that direction. The result is that people know what they are about; similarities and differences can be talked about. Opinions osmose instead of forming cataracts, so ironically individuals have more freedom in that 'ism' climate than in the bogus 'non-ism' we have to deal with here. A 'school' exists in this country, but it doesn't call itself a school and that is the problem. The mainstream is a school (perhaps the fact is hidden because of all its annexes and split sites) and not just a convenient label for the centre. Its original curriculum was laid out in the 50s by the Movement, but since then it has let in any pupil who passes the 'mannerism' exam and wears the 'naturalism' tie – even Rap then gets through on a scholarship, along with the girls from Fem Street Primary. And the post-mod boys from Irony Prep go straight into top-stream.

So where is poetry heading in this country? Another way of asking the same question would be to ask what the rate of change will be for this endemic school that doesn't call itself a school. I don't particularly care. I just want its stranglehold on word-creativity to be blown away, or at least for that stranglehold to be discussed openly again. Are poets in opposing camps really going to leave it to the literary historians to carry out a ghostly conversation for them?

The immediately visible difference between *most* of the modernists and *most* of the mainstream is that the modernists deal with the problem of language itself, while the mainstream, for a host of reasons (some ultimately political) doesn't. This cuts our mainstream off from the 'mainstream' of late 20th Century intellectual enquiry, making it a piddly anachronism relative to the world's mainstream. *Most* of it follows models which utilise language as a given tool for 'expressing yourself' in a way that many of us find 'dull' in both senses of the word – as in 'boring' and as in 'stupid'.

Many of the other differences are subsets of the 'language' thing anyway: the area of representation *vs* abstraction; referential *vs* non-referential; portraying life *vs* changing life; spontaneity *vs* construction etc. Ironically, these debates, where you would think at least one polarity was the concern of the mainstream, are confined to innovative circles. The mainstream has shut the door on so much by its limited preoccupations, that it doesn't even want to get itself into first gear. It goes on talking about the effective or ineffective methods for communicating expressed 'subject', while the rest of the world rushes on in 5th. There are big debates going on out there and poetry, as *the* pivotal language artform, has in the long term more to contribute to them than anything else.

So all-in-all the picture is bleak. The future lies with the young, as it always does, but young English poets are inundated with reductive models of writing and when they stray towards something 'other' they generally do so in a vacuum. The future of poetry is not to be found in 1990s UK.

What do you think poetry is capable of?

I know it is capable of giving me a series of 'intense' experiences and that these experiences are unique to reading poetry. I'm talking here of reading other's poetry by the way. In some poems, that experience is a matter of degree – it is more or it is less – but there are other poems where the experience is not just less, but fundamentally of a different kind.

I also listen to what others say about reading poetry and I get the impression I am not the only one who gets an intense experience sometimes. And often the material that gives another that experience is the same material that I respond to – sometimes not – sometimes the match is different.

It is because I know what some poetry is capable of that I get irritated when a poetry is championed, which for me, does less, particularly when in the same breath the material I go for is slagged.

Now I don't want that intensity all the time, I couldn't handle it, but in general it is what I go to poetry for. I don't go to it for the same things I might go to TV, fiction, films or songs for, though there is a cross-over with painting and music. I tend not to go to it for opinion or anecdote or stuff that I will look for in, what for me, are more suitable mediums. I go for the kick – that pleasure-rush that language (the combination of the cerebral, physical, intellectual and emotional in words), when used creatively, is capable of inducing.

Are you interested in poetry as a process or as a product? Are your poems and books objects or subjects?

Wow! – process or product? One is usually foregrounded, for ideological or aesthetic reasons, at the expense of the other. To begin with, we have process

– the process of a single writer's development and the process of their single poems. But these are determined by pre-existing products – poems that a writer has read and liked or disliked, poems that those in 'authority' have said are good or bad etc. The sequence is PRODUCT > PROCESS > PRODUCT > METAPROCESS.

What is important about this, how this question relates to poetics, is the way in which the value of product is, in current mainstream practice, devaluing process to such a damaging extent. Process has essentially been prematurely robbed of its energy in order to feed the vampire product. This is what lies behind the domination of what I call 'The Workshop School'. The situation behind the Workshop domination is simple. It is where the guide-lines for new poets – those things said to them by the creative writing tutor to stop them making initial errors – become the precepts for ALL poetry. The workshop is concerned with the creation of a product – something as close as possible to the 'publishable-and-makes-no-mistakes' poem. This has become the norm and at the expense of the kind of messy, long-term, hit and miss, chancy processes that if left to develop have the *real* potential. It was the Workshop school, not the Martians, who were the real movers in the 80s and the plethora of domestic anecdote and bourgeois biographics we have been inundated with since is the result.

A related anomaly is this work's so-called clinging to 'individual experience' – the result is hundreds of poems which could have been written by one person and, in a way, they have: a kind of English 90s Everyperson. The domination of this hidden formalism through the medium of a bogus subjectivism becomes particularly evident when you discover that 50% of the material is fiction anyway – but they are poems written in such a way that a reader actually believes the stuff is real; then the poet smiles smugly and says in quiet astonishment 'No, no, it didn't actually happen.' And again, what 'didn't actually happen' has happened to us all, at least twice a week. This is the Workshop School's towering achievement and many poets are locked in that tower.

Your own poetry has become increasingly radical over the past few years. Why?

Boredom with my own voice basically. I've never been interested in writing poems that could have been written by someone else, but I have always been interested in poems that could have been written by other Me's. And I love the idea of poems that could not have been written by either me or anyone else. The whole thing is a paradox anyway. All my poems are mine – however much I might imagine that what I am writing is not 'me', they always are – the themes come through, but they come through expanded. 'I is another' – how did that teenage scrap from the Ardennes over a century ago know so much? There are more particular reasons. For years I wrote indecipherable prose-poetry jigsaws in notebooks. Then they ran out and I used cheap A4 pads which I split into two long halves – the poems would always start at the top and finish at the bottom. With this new attention to 'line' came a desire to 'say things' again – use my philosophic meanderings as 'material'. For years the bulk of my poetry had been oneiric – creating texture and experience, but I needed to move on. The results were unexpected: the combination produced a poetry much less straightforward in its 'thoughts' and a lot more problematic with structure. It was exhilarating.

Then I began 'writing' directly onto computer. Ironically, this cold application ran parallel with an increased emotional and personal element in my writing. I was also using chance again, but to a greater degree than ever before. I got into the habit a long time ago of destroying mood. It is so easy to create a mood in a poem and yet I'd hear workshop tutors going on about how vital it was – tosh. I'd draw in something to deliberately veer the poem off in another direction.

I was also reading a lot more innovative poetry as, being an editor, material which before I only got hold of occasionally by accident, was suddenly all around me. For the first time in years I was being influenced too, particularly by innovative American poetry. I'd almost missed out on a whole decade of experimental work from the USA, the 80s. So when I picked up the *Up Late* anthology around 1990 it blew me away – it was there I first read people like Lyn Hejinian and Susan Howe etc. There was next to nothing in the book – and it was a big book – that I never responded to positively: late New York School, Post-Vietnam Dada, Talk Poetry, Neo-primitivism, Urban Romantics, Language. And there were always those flashes of hybrid-surrealism – work which worshipped the imagination, but was distinctly materialist. The work was expansive, open to the modern world, relaxed yet dense. Something had been going on, but it took me a few years to discover just how intense that 'going on' was. Some of the poets introduced to me there have since become great favourites.

The most direct influence has to be down to the way many of the more radical of them employ syntactic innovation for what, at first appearance, seems to be in the cause of an extra-dimensional lyricism. In the early 80s I was writing stuff where being violent with syntax was a form of expressionism, but this was different. I was now finding myself disordering for the sake of a sense of beauty: find an ugly cliche line from a poem by Everyperson, rearrange it, take out the word 'brother' and put 'ear-drop' in its place, juggle the conjunctions, verbalise the subject noun – create – give – give away – throw away – discover –

rediscover – lose – replace buried treasure. Images bloom where before was only factoid. Texture vibrates where before was only worktop. And as I've said before, as long as you lie through your teeth in good faith, the truth will trickle through – new truth. That's one side of it anyway.

BINARY MYTHS 2
correspondences with poet-editors

Introduction

British poetry exists in multiform states at present – probably more so than it has ever done – and this diversity of writing practice is reflected in the publications that exist to represent it. This book is, first of all, an acknowledgement of this diversity. However, this very same diversity raises some contentious points, not least the often-voiced complaint that poetry proliferates to the point of distraction: who could possibly hope to sift through the ever-burgeoning piles of magazines, pamphlets, anthologies and individual collections? Given that the readership is little more than the number of poets producing poems; that poets are generally the main readers of other poets' work and that poetry itself is super-abundant, what are the motivations of publishing houses and poetry editors? How do they select work? What do they select? What do they choose to leave out, or to leave to others and why? Why do we need more poetry books?

These are simple, but vital questions with a recent historical background, given the exclusive nature of much high-profile poetry publishing in the past and, conversely, the explosion of small presses which came with the availability of cheap means of reproduction and, more recently, the advent of desktop publishing. This has improved the quality of some small press productions to the standards of the well-established and well-funded major presses. Many of these small ventures continue to be enervating and innovative enterprises, carrying forward the radical energies and interests of many of the early small presses. These questions are also questions for the future – linked to questions surrounding electronic publishing – which may help to identify some of the ways in which poets and publishers might work if we are to continue to enjoy a broad base to British poetry and a rational debate between its elements.

Binary Myths 2 explores such questions with a group of contemporary poet-editors. They range from those who edit high-profile poetry lists for large publishing houses, through the editors of small press publishing houses, to editors of poetry magazines and those who have edited single influential volumes or anthologies. This book does not attempt to be an exhaustive list of all current British poet-editors, rather a sample from the contemporary crop. Some high-profile poet-editors were invited to contribute, but could not afford the time in busy working schedules to take part in the project; some were invited and found they had to pull out due to other work pressures. The editor of an excellent recent anthology of Black-British poets declined to take part, commenting that he would have no need of poetry itself if the necessary statements could be made in articles such as these. Others also felt that they had nothing to add to any debates about poetry, whether their own work, or work which they have edited. Still others are absent because of the limits of space, although the broad kinds of poetry that they publish (or have edited) is represented in this book by other poet-editors of similar persuasions. Finally, some poetry editors are not themselves poets and, therefore, fell outside the remit of this project: some questions were purposefully asked to open up a debate on the ways in which editing, writing and reading might inform each other.

It is hoped therefore that, whilst there are gaps, the overall spread of interests covers much of the current poetry map: from the avant-garde and linguistically innovative, to the broadly accessible mainstream; from the editors of best-selling, panacean Women's Anthologies, to small press reviews magazines; from the editors of small press publishing houses, to the majors. As such, this is a companion volume to *Binary Myths: conversations with contemporary poets.* Both books attempt to investigate the divisions and polarities in contemporary poetic thinking and practice, by engaging with a spread of radically different practitioners. Both books also aim to introduce a climate of reasoned debate between these multifarious elements and go some way to removing obstructive oppositions that are based on simplistic binary arguments.

Since beginning this *Binary Myths* project in 1996, it strikes me that there has been a shift (at some levels, at least, in the workings of British poetry), towards a more pluralistic critique. Such a shift can be seen in the reception of *Binary Myths* itself; the generous editorial of *Poetry Review* Vol 86 No 3, which featured work by (and articles about) Modernist and Postmodernist poets, the avant-garde, and an intelligent review of *Conductors of Chaos* by Ian Sansom, that puts other 'anyone-can-do-that' reviews to shame. Other shifts include John Kinsella's and Michael Hulse's appointment as the new editors of *Stand*, which has already included an intelligently diverse range of writing. There has also been a general broadening of editorial selection in both the small press – Stride, Slow Dancer and Arc stand out as three excellent examples – and in large mainstream presses, which now include a greater plurality of poets. One need only look at the inclusion of the following 'innovative writers' on mainstream lists to see how far improved the situation is: Tom Leonard at Cape; Ian Duhig, Maggie Hannan, W.N. Herbert, Douglas Oliver, Tom Pickard, J.H. Prynne, Peter Reading (and others) at Bloodaxe; Miles Champion, Michael Haslam, John Riley (and others) at Carcanet . Each of these shifts – and all it takes is a shift in critical discussion and perception – surely points up the fact that the days of Them-and-Us separatism and uncritical fighting are over. If they are not over, is it certainly not time that they were?

The same approach has been taken for both books: the project was conducted through correspondence, giving each of the poet-editors the chance to answer the same or similar questions, or to choose from them the areas of enquiry which were of most interest to them. Some have answered the questions directly; others have taken a more tangential look at the issues raised and contributed pieces that reflect the questions in their writing/editorial lives. After their initial responses, in most cases, we continued a short correspondence to pick up on recurring themes, or to explore emerging avenues. A list of the initial questions is reproduced at the end of the book.

The poet-editors have all engaged in these correspondences with candour and enthusiasm and I am deeply grateful to them all for their interest and support.

Andy Brown, July 1999

Gillian Allnutt

I didn't think, when I agreed to take part in this project, that it is ten years since I have worked as an editor and that my ideas in that time have changed a great deal.

From 1983 – 1988 I was poetry editor at *City Limits* magazine. Every week I produced half a page of listings; notes on competitions, events, controversies; a review or two; a picture. Of course *City Limits* was an alternative to everything, even *Time Out*, and I made it my business to cover those poets and performers – women poets, gay poets, black poets, working-class poets – not published by mainstream presses or reviewed in mainstream newspapers and journals. I turned down offers from bright young white men to write reviews and gave myself a lot of extra work seeking out women and ethnic minority writers with the confidence to review and a prose style that would at least meet halfway the prevailing white, male, Oxbridge-educated prose of the magazine.

In 1988 I co-edited *The New British Poetry 1968 -1988* published by Paladin. I compiled the section of women poets; Fred D'Aguiar did Black British poets; Eric Mottram did older experimental poets and Ken Edwards the younger experimental poets. It made for an odd mixture. I was glad to 'give away' black and experimental women poets to other sections, in order to have as many women as possible in the anthology. I put nineteen poets into my allotted 60 pages. I chose poets whose work I liked and wished to put forward. I think they were supposed to be 'feminist' poets, but I opted for 'women'. John Muckle, the overall editor, named the section 'Quote Feminist Unquote Poetry'. Since then, some of the poets have become more public, some less.

In late 1988 I moved to the North East of England and was invited to join the editorial collective of *Writing Women* magazine. I worked on the magazine for six months before remembering why I'd moved out of London and into my chosen 'exile' in the North East. It wasn't just to take on more of the same work I'd been doing in the South, but to undertake the much more difficult work of sorting myself out.

In many ways, this was a work of 'un-editing': it involved discarding the 'received' version of my own history in order to uncover the 'real'. In the course of therapy I kept a journal I called 'Garble and Blurb'. Garble was a tall, thin man and Blurb a short, fat one and they argued it all out with each other on scrap paper and I let them. I never tried to shut them up, though they were an odd pair and not very PC. Their legacy is a sheaf of new ideas – many of them red rags to the ageing Lefty in me – and a residual distrust of being right about anything.

What processes lie behind the writing of your poems?

1. Teaching Creative Writing

Since 1983 I have been teaching creative writing in groups, classes and workshops in a wide variety of contexts, working with both adults and children. I always get people to write in the sessions. Always with adults and sometimes with children, I also write myself, doing whatever I've asked everyone else to do. And, along with everyone else, I read out what I've written. I feel it is important, in the interests of trust, to lay myself on the line in this way. Doing this has led to a change in the way I write poems. In order to have something coherent enough to read out after, say, half an hour's writing time in a workshop, I write in prose. When I get home, if I think there's something there, I work from the prose to a poem, beginning by chopping up the prose into one sentence per line in a rough, typed, first draft. Poems that don't start in workshops don't start in prose. The advent of beginning-with-prose has seemed like a big change to me, but I'm not sure it really is.

2. Doing Psychotherapy

'Know thyself' has probably always been one of my chief motivations for writing. (I also love messing about with words). Of course I was afraid that doing therapy would put paid to writing poetry. But it opened doors and helped me go deeper into myself. While I was doing therapy I found myself writing nearly all the time 'in persona' and loving the freedom of being anyone other than myself. I got interested in history, not just my own. I became aware, through drawing and painting, of the pictures in my poetry. I hadn't understood that I thought so much in pictures. I learned much more about how to let poems, like dreams, show me where I am about to go. I learned to read and interpret them.

3. Doing the Writing

I have worked in concentrated bursts on poems, five or six hours or more at a time, and usually managed to finish them all in one go. Occasionally I have felt that my brain would explode in the attempt to forge or fathom some new connection contained in a poem. I suspect that this way of working was dependent on smoking to sustain concentration. Now I have given up, I have to imagine unimaginable new ways of working on poems.

What important influences have shaped your current interests?

T.S. Eliot, Hopkins, George Herbert, Donne, Plath, Emily Dickinson, Emily Brontë, Tsvetayeva, Akhmatova, Hardy, Anglo-Saxon poetry.

What are you reading at present?

In a word, everything. One of the best results of therapy has been the gift of reading. Now I am open, now I can read voraciously in a way I've always wanted to. So I am catching up, even attempting some keeping up. I'm reading 14th Century poets in connection with a projected sequence of poems about Julian of Norwich. I'm reading contemporary poetry, mainly British and Irish, and contemporary fiction. I'm reading men, because for years I read mainly women. Right now I'm reading contemporary Polish poetry, because I'm about to go on a British Council expedition to Poland.

Should poetry be difficult, or should poets make their work easily understandable?

Right at the beginning of my teaching career in further and adult education, I learned that people, no matter what their level of education, respond to 'good' rather than 'accessible' poetry. Twenty-six years on, this still appears to be the case. I can't believe that it has to do only with my own body-language, with the way I have presented various poems to groups of students.

I remember one occasion, in the 70s, when I took a set of David Holbrook's *Iron Honey Gold* anthologies (published in the early 60s) into a class and asked the (adult) students to find a poem they liked. A woman from a Caribbean island picked John Clare's 'Written in Northampton County Asylum'. It was not a choice I would have predicted. I remember, because it was so moving, her talking about a child of hers that had died. I guess it was the overwhelming sadness in Clare's poem that touched her, in spite of the slight stiffness and oddness of the language.

On the other hand, two years ago I found myself concluding a review of *The Forward Book of Poetry 1997* with these words: 'This is an anthology I shall not be ashamed to circulate among the least well-read of creative writing classes.' That was because it contained very little of what I sometimes suspect to be deliberately obfuscatory poetry: poetry whose difficulty is there in order to show the cleverness of the poet and not much else; poetry, it almost seems to me, designed to make the reader feel an idiot.

I don't think poets need to be presented with 'shoulds' as to the nature of their work. But my own 'should' would be this: a poem should be only as difficult as it needs to be. A couple of years ago, someone in a writers' group (a bumptious man, it must be said) reproached me with the difficulty of some of the work in *Nantucket and the Angel*. My response was: 'Well, I didn't do it on purpose.' I'm not sure that was entirely true. The sequence 'Nantucket and the Angel' *does* show off, *is* clever rather than intelligent a lot of the time, and I don't feel entirely comfortable with that. But there are poems in the sequence which are probably difficult to read because they were very difficult to write and I make no apology for those.

I think love comes into the question of what degree of difficulty in a poet's work any reader is prepared to contend with. T.S.Eliot, Elizabeth Bishop, the contemporary Canadian poet Erin Mouré: I've persevered with all of them, because each has carried me into that poetry space about which Tomas Tranströmer once said in an interview: 'Thank God I can breathe here.' There are other poets whose work – regardless of how much admired it is by others – I know will never do that for me and so it's not worth wrestling with its difficulty.

But please, please, in a time that would dumb us all down, don't make poetry easy. Don't abolish Geoffrey Hill. Let there be some peripheral place where we may engage with a level of emotional and spiritual maturity hardly permitted to flourish anywhere else.

What is the point of an anthology?

1. It could help keep an academic in his/her post.
2. It could feed our pre-millenial hunger for overviews.
3. It could make a publishing house appear non-racist, non-sexist etc.: 'Look, we've done women poets, gay poets, black poets, Scottish poets.'
4. Inclusion in an anthology or two helps a new writer towards his/her first individual collection.

From the reader's point of view – or rather my own:

Iron Honey Gold – Ed. David Holbrook, 4 Volumes, Cambridge University Press, 1965; *Come Hither* – Ed. Walter de la Mare, 2 Volumes, Puffin, 1973.

I love both of these anthologies because they are personal choices based on love (and, in Holbrook's case, what's good for you, but it's palatable). And neither editor is bashing you over the head with the hammer of classification.

The Bloodaxe Book of Contemporary Women Poets – Ed. Jeni Couzyn, Bloodaxe, 1985.

240 pages and only eleven poets – good. A decent selection of poems, a photo and an autobiographical essay (biographical in the case of Stevie Smith and Sylvia Plath) for each one. This gives you a solid sense of each poet. And I've found in the last couple of years, reviewing Adcock, Fainlight, Feinstein, say, it's been a great book to go back to, to re-read some of their earlier work and find something autobiographical to help contextualise the new collection.

Penguin Anthologies of poetry from different periods of English Literature, eg: *The Metaphysical Poets* – Ed. Helen Gardner, Penguin, 1957.

Very useful if you're a poet without a degree in Eng. Lit. You can sound knowledgeable on comparatively little reading, or be helped to find your way in to those poets you really like, or both.

The Forward Book of Poetry 1997
Being asked to review this at the end of 1996 coincided with the beginning of my own attempt to get back in touch with contemporary poetry and it was a brilliant way of finding out what was newly published and what, out of that, I particularly wanted to pursue.

I rarely read poetry anthologies for pleasure. I find them, like magazines and anthologies of short stories, bitty and disjointed. I read them to find out what there is to read and/or what I ought to read or know about. They provide a short cut to the literature of an epoch, a country, a sex, a race. I can't be bothered with those that are published to prove a theory or create a controversy.

We live in a visually-biased, image-based culture; how does this affect your work?

Our image-based culture must adversely affect the reception that all poets get, because if people are less in the habit of visualising what is given to them in words, poetry will be less readily available to them. Who was it said that the pictures are better on the radio?

When I was poetry editor at *City Limits*, I went to a great many poetry readings and, after a while, I realised that my own listening skills had improved. I have also learned to listen because of teaching creative writing and having to say something intelligent about students' writing on only one hearing. And I listen to the radio a lot; I don't have a television. Even so, I don't rate my ability to listen especially. We no longer read aloud to one another at home (I love Radio 4's *Book at Bedtime*), nor do we entertain one another with conversational storytelling. In Ireland I have realised that in England we have lost the pleasure of finding inventive, intriguing, amusing ways of telling things around the table, or even at the bus stop.

Living in an image-based culture doesn't stop me thinking about the 'sound' side of poetry. I miss the attention that might have been paid to sound in the work of contemporary poets. I pay a lot of attention to it in my own work. That's probably because I feel much closer to music than to visual art. I love music, know a bit about it and have played various instruments: it matters to me.

By not focussing on the 'sound' side of poetry, we miss out on the pre-verbal elements in language and so lose a great deal. We are so hell-bent on 'understanding' – the cognitive, analytical understanding of the left brain – that we miss out on the 'knowing' – the intuitive knowing of the right brain – that might come to us through the drama of rhythm and patterns of sound. How much have we gained, how much lost, by translating the Bible into the bald-bland-speak of the late 20th Century?

Why still publish books in the 'electronic age'?

1. Whoever breaks into your house is not going to take the books.
2. Books will still work on 1st January 2000.
3. Books, like the trees they are made from, are friends.
4. Even though they are now printed photographically – or electronically? – you can touch the words in a book.
5. Nothing on screen has a body.

Neil Astley

What's going on in contemporary poetry that interests you? Is poetry in a healthy state at the moment, or is it heading nowhere? Is contemporary poetry a divided thing? Divided which ways? How are you bridging the gaps?

I'd like begin answering this by quoting a response from another interview. This is Douglas Oliver, replying to a question from Patrick Wright on a recent Radio 3 *Postscript* programme called *Outriders* (1 February 1999):

> I don't think that poetry in modern Britain is occupying its full public space. What you might call the 'populist' wing of poetry is concerned to attract a particular audience which doesn't really like poetry of a broader political face but really wants poetry to reflect their own personal lives, and what it's like to have that kind of personal life if you're a poet; and wants to be entertained and have a certain amount of humour and human incident or to have particular topics presented in a poetic way. That's what you might call the 'populist' wing. Whereas the highly sophisticated 'experimental' wing of poetry is very preoccupied with modern philosophical problems of just such questions as public space and is trying to tackle the difficulties of language itself and the possibility of making an innovative language which will create its own new sense of political meaning. My heart is with a poetry which is various, and which is sufficiently various to represent the modern city but also sufficiently various to represent all the different possibilities and faculties of the human mind.

As an editor straddling several different 'camps' and someone geographically as well as emotionally and culturally distanced from the metropolitan pub talking-shop of literary politics, I share Oliver's sense of unease at the current position of contemporary poetry, which is both divided (but when has it not been?) as well as in a state of flux, although my loyalties aren't as weighted towards some of the writers he admires. In answering some of these questions, I think it's important to cast my answers in terms of poetry *readership*, for while there is much to admire in much of the poetry being published now, I think there's now a danger that many poets and editors are becoming so obsessed with personal reputations and canon-making that they risk alienating their readers and also risk losing sight of their own poetic vision. Because I think contemporary poetry is in a state of flux, my response to Oliver's characterisation has to be ambiguous, for I think he is both right and wrong in what he says, about readers as well as about poets, for neither is a homogenous species.

I think it's true that unlike many writers of earlier generations, most of today's published poets have their feet planted firmly in the 'real world', usually working as freelance writers. Although some have part-time teaching commitments, most try to make a living of sorts from readings, workshops, schools work, residencies, fellowships, commissions of various kinds and literary journalism, or from writing the mainstream novels or non-fiction books which support the rest of their writing. The poet can be paid to do almost anything relating to poetry, it seems, but rarely just to write it; and yet while these poets are seen as more in touch with the wider world, the pressures of the 'poetry business' are such that many feel themselves becoming less centred as poets.

The more self-aware realise that they must sometimes try to ignore economic need in order to give priority to the basic need all poets have for time in which to consider, re-think and re-charge as well as simply to write. Poets have spoken to me of the adverse effects of giving numerous public readings of the same poems: that the language and structures of those poems start to 'imprint' themselves over attempts to write new work; as with public expectation for a writer to keep producing certain kinds of poetry, there is a danger of pastiche or self-parody. In many ways this is not a new phenomenon – one sees it, for example, affecting the later work of Dylan Thomas – but it is a potentially debilitating side effect of today's poetry business on the poetry itself, one which affects even the youngest writers.

With the poets pressured by the 'business', their attention distracted by the personalities of the poetry network or marketplace, and without the time and space in which to read and absorb the work of other writers, as well as to experiment with possible new directions for their own work, is it any wonder that many talented newcomers don't develop their poetry beyond one or two tricks, so that you can often identify perhaps only half a dozen narrative structures which characterise virtually all their poems, while older poets start feeling less inclined to push forward with the next collection when they see these younger upstarts getting all the critical and media attention?

Wordsworth wrote of poets creating the taste by which their work should be judged. That's certainly the case with the great poet, but there are only a handful of those in any century. Then you have the new, original voice, the poet who's writing unlike anyone else, but only a handful come along in any decade. In that category, from the Bloodaxe list, I would put poets such as David Constantine, Peter Didsbury, Selima Hill, Peter Reading, Ken Smith and Pauline Stainer; and from other lists, John Burnside, Paul Durcan, Medbh McGuckian, Paul Muldoon and Alice Oswald. These are poets whose work is so distinctive that their voice, music and formal sense are unmistakably their own not just in every collection but in every poem. I think of them – and several others – as poets whom readers might sometimes need to be educated (in the sense of the Latin *educere*, to lead or draw out) to appreciate, but also as the exceptions.

One of the main factors which inhibits that 'education' process for the general reader is that poetry reviewing in the national press has become impoverished in impact and content. Despite the fact that more people are buying and reading poetry, newspaper literary editors are giving less space to poetry than to books which command a much smaller following (because of subject or price) and not only publishing poetry reviews less often but not printing them until several months after a book has appeared, by which time the bookshops have returned their unsold stock to the publisher's warehouse.

When you read some of these reviews, you might perhaps excuse the literary editor on the grounds that such writing should be left in a tray until it can be cut to fit a space or column, but not when you read the books, or when, as the publisher, you already know them. But literary editors – like the readers of their newspapers – get their sense of the new poetry books, and their importance, relevance or otherwise, from the reviews. And to re-phrase Adrian Mitchell: most poetry readers ignore most poetry books because most poetry reviewers ignore both book and reader.

With a few honourable exceptions, most of the poetry reviewers in the national press don't even review the poetry, for they don't review it for the reader. They don't give the reader an illuminating account of the book which will make them want to read it themselves, nor do they give any impression of caring about the poetry, so that the reader isn't even touched by the excitement or passionate engagement evident in the reviewer's response to the work. Instead they present an opinionated assessment of the book in which they sound off in a grudging fashion about what they dislike about the poetry, or what the poet should or shouldn't have done, often subjecting the work to a complete demolition job (given the shortage of space that poetry receives, wouldn't ignoring that book and writing about another instead be much more helpful?). And as if that weren't bad enough, the review is so ridden with jargon, niggles, put-downs, smart remarks and quotations plucked out of context to support an abstruse argument, that no one outside the reviewer's inner circle of poet-friends can get any sense of the particular distinctive qualities of the book supposedly being reviewed for the benefit of the reader of the newspaper. Even when the review is positive, the reader isn't led towards the book, but feels shut out from it. And because the amount of space given to poetry is so little now, one paragraph in this kind of arrogant and patronising review may be the only notice given in the national press to a book which – if it's a Selected or Collected

Poems – may represent the life's work of one poet, an incredible insult to the poet as well as to the reader.

I said earlier that there were some poets I thought of as exceptions in terms of reader response. So where does that leave all the others? In my view, it means that while a poet may not write 'for' readers, it's the readership which justifies publication. All editors are flooded with submissions of poetry from people whose desire to be published is greater than their desire to write well, which must involve reading the work of poets from all periods, but few seem to grasp that if you don't read poetry, you can't expect to be able to write poetry of any value – poetry which other people will want to read. And yet the ego is similarly rampant even amongst published poets: the bogus poetry personality cult which takes the focus of public and media attention away from the poetry and into the not-very-interesting (to others) lives, loves, hates, grudges and petty vendettas of the networking poets and their hangers-on. Witness the recent press coverage of *Birthday Letters*, the Laureateship, the Faber poetry editorship and the Gormenghastian machinations at Oxford University Press: no need to discuss the poetry when you have the poets and the poetry business to chew over.

How do you select work for a poetry list? Should poetry lists demonstrate consistency, or diversity? Given that poetry in general falls short of audience numbers and big book sales, what should be the motivating forces of poetry publishing?

These questions take me back to Douglas Oliver's advocacy of a poetry which is various. When critics tackle me about about Bloodaxe, their usual charge is 'Bloodaxe publishes too many books'. But Bloodaxe is the reader's publisher, offering high quality work right across the diverse range of contemporary poetry. Poetry lists which are too narrow are never sustainable, and Bloodaxe has been strengthened over the years in being able to take on 'refugees' from commercial houses who weren't able or willing to maintain their once vibrant poetry lists. With an output of up to 40 poetry books a year, Bloodaxe does the work of two or more publishers. If Bloodaxe didn't publish 'too many books', readers and poets would suffer. At the same time, I look for consistency within a diverse list.

Poetry critics and reviewers are often frustrated censors. If you list the poets repeatedly mentioned by them in essays and reviews, or in their anthologies they edit, you will find that each is wanting to establish his (and it is usually his) own limited list of approved writers, whether it's the Western Canon of Harold Bloom, the Helen Vendler Pantheon, the Sean O'Brien Politburo, the Michael

Schmidt Curriculum, the New Plain Stylists of Peter Forbes, or what Andrew Motion and Blake Morrison and 'a number of close observers have come to think of as the new British poetry'. In many cases the poets picked for these teams defy the selection criteria, so that you have poets represented in many anthologies by unrepresentative work (which is unhelpful to readers and students as well as to the poets), while Postmodern poets find they aren't Postmodern after all when their work is the subject of an editorial in *Poetry Review*.

I feel that my responsibility as a poetry publisher is not to critics and reviewers but to poets and their readership.

Bloodaxe has always challenged the literary establishment. I don't accept that tastes and reputations should be dictated by out-of-touch professors with literary critical hang-ups or reviewers more concerned with fashion than excellence. In making the best new poetry available to readers, through bookshops and through actively promoting poetry on radio, television and in the papers, we have been able to by-pass the critics. In the past, writers had to have critical acceptance before their work could reach a wide readership. This is no longer the case. We've published many poets who've sold thousands of books before critics have even started to *think* about writing about them.

Yes, I admit it, I have risked my reputation for twenty years by publishing many first collections, including those by Simon Armitage, David Constantine, Peter Didsbury, Ian Duhig, Helen Dunmore, Jackie Kay, Glyn Maxwell, Sean O'Brien and Pauline Stainer, to name a few who have continued to produce the goods. And I would stand by my decision to publish other first collections by writers whose subsequent work has not lived up to their early promise. But this is often the case with poets, who will cram ten excited years of living and thinking into that first book, and then try to outdo that achievement for the second collection in a much shorter period, often with their lives and focus changed by the mere fact of the first book's publication or by the pressures of the competitive 'poetry business'. If I feel that the second book is a pale imitation of the first, I will try to work with them to help build up a stronger second collection, which often means encouraging them to take more time, to be patient and to try to regain their focus (to shut out the clutter of the literary world), but if the poet's sense of his or her reputation has become stronger than the poetry that reputation is meant to be founded upon, the editorial relationship will have broken down irretrievably, and the poet goes off to court new admirers.

Should poetry be difficult, or should poets make their work more easily understandable? Does good poetry sell, or popular poetry? Does popular really mean good?

Poetry has varying degrees of difficulty, but it's the publisher's job (and in an ideal world, the reviewer's!) to make their work more easily understandable to as wide a readership as possible, through imaginative marketing and specialised kinds of publicity.

Access and accessibility are two of the current buzzwords of arts administration, but too often the response of what's called the 'provider' is not to give an audience access to challenging work but to give them what Douglas Oliver would characterise as 'what they already know', or worse, to patronise them with second-rate or diluted forms of poetry. If they want entertainment or stand-up, that's fine, but don't protect them from the real thing.

In any year, Bloodaxe's output will include several books of 'difficult' poetry. In this respect, I think it's important both to serve the existing readership of such writers, and to do everything possible to broaden their appeal to as wide a readership as possible. And ideally I'd like to see the reverse happening, for I think any readers who've bought Bloodaxe titles by poets such as J.H. Prynne, Jacques Dupin and Douglas Oliver would find much to admire also in the poetry of G.F. Dutton, W.N. Herbert, Maggie Hannan and Ian Duhig.

Through publishing Prynne, I've become more aware of the breadth of his influence, which seems to me to run outside the experimental wing which claims him as their own, like an underground seeping out of the 'underground'. In a way, Prynne's texts stand as a kind of pure poetry, a condition to which other poetry aspires, but the contemporary poets who interest me most are not those who imitate their models (whether they be Prynne, or Plath, Hughes, Larkin, Harrison or Muldoon) but those who learn from them. Poets as different as Barry MacSweeney, Philip Gross and John Kinsella have learned from Prynne. And when you examine Prynne's often bizarre subject-matter, his mixing of diction from ancient texts and from scientific discourse, his juxtaposition of the languages of politics, economics and consumerism in poetry written over 20 years ago, you wonder how many more of the 'populist' poets he has influenced, either directly or through the work of other poets who have read him.

The poetry divisions are artificial. What purpose do they serve? Like all artificial rules, they're there to be broken.

One of the benefits of having a diverse list is that publishing more popular poets helps 'subsidise' the publication of the more difficult poets, whose books will sell but more slowly and not always through mainstream outlets. But this method of supporting difficult work isn't just a phenomenon of the 'subsidised' poetry publishing sector: Faber have always published Ezra Pound at a loss and I imagine they've 'carried' writers such as W.S. Graham as well, as a service to readers.

Tilla Brading

What is going on in contemporary poetry that interests you? Is poetry in a healthy state at the moment or is it heading nowhere?

There's so much going on that interests me, but I have to go in search of it through libraries, databases, conferences, galleries, small press magazines and second-hand bookshops, or bump into it accidentally as well as finding it around me. This is because the best buzz I get from poetry isn't presented to me on High Street shelves or in poetry tour promotions. I can enjoy these too, but think (because, hell, I can't define or fix anything) what I find most exciting at the moment is three-dimensional work. By this I mean work that has a physical presence, or dimension perhaps like a performance – not a reading, incidentally – a performance using the whole body and maybe visuals and sound too. Or it may be three-dimensional in the sculptural, installation sense. Or it may be sculptural on the page, making the words create their own meaning, working like paint or clay. What I gain from it is a whole response, almost physical, sensual and sexual.

I'm also interested in what poetry is on the Internet, but as yet I'm rather ignorant of what's available as I am limited by infrequent access to this and e-mail.

I also like to know what's going on across the whole spectrum, so welcome the books which come for review at *PQR*, local readings, the people who come to creative writing courses and the High Street selection. But, generally, these don't excite me like the kind of work I've outlined above. I prefer subtlety to statement and like to be intellectually stimulated by language, image, metaphor, idea etc.

To interest me, if it isn't 3-D, then poetry has got to work well in the way it sets out to create that connection with the reader, which the reader recognises. It's as old as human nature I expect, experienced when 'A marvel befell me, as might a fairy-tale' (Langland). It's survival bodes well for the future – the continual survival of a poetic sensibility.

So the poet / artists who most interest me are those who get labelled in some of the following ways: innovative, boundary breaking, language, book-works, performance-art, concrete, installation, interactive, cyber, theatre, body-art... Anthologies such as *Conductors of Chaos* (Iain Sinclair, Picador), *A State of Independence* (Tony Frazer, Stride), or *Out of Everywhere* (Maggie O'Sullivan, Reality Street). Publishers such as Reality Street, Maquette, Writer's Forum, Graeme Murray, Sound & Language; individuals; magazines such as *Angel Exhaust, Shearsman, Terrible Work, Oasis, Gare du Nord, Écorché.*

The last magazine fascinates rather than interests me. Violence, with which it deals (and especially violence against the body), I find disturbing. It even makes me nervous. But that is part of its fascination – if a work is creating this response in me, even if I don't like it, then it's creating something vital – I don't have to like it, perhaps I should feel revulsion – unless I become a sadist or masochist...?

A different fascination, rather than enjoyment, is what I gain from those poets who, while using words as a medium like plasticine, constrict, solidify and tighten it to shut out the reader. This, it seems, is its wonder. It reveals a fundamental tightening of language which I admire, which interests me, but which shuts me out.

So I find a lot that's healthy, if healthy means vibrant, living, changing, exploring. I also see a lot that, for me, is heading nowhere, but I know there'll always be people who want to go nowhere with it. There's room for everyone.

Are you interested in hybridizing poetries or hybridizing poetry with other art forms?

The word 'hybridizing' could be taken two ways: either within poetry styles and forms, or between poetry and other art forms, such as art and sculpture.

The first instance could blur and merge performance, rap, traditional, language, sonnets and so on. I think it's healthy and exciting to blur boundaries and create new mixes and modes of expression. However, if that was taken too far then each kind of work could splurge across the other and create a conglomerate where every piece was much the same. I like difference and newness, so like to see a variety of styles even if some of them aren't my scene. The differences are what stimulate and give variety. By concentrating on one style at a time, a poet can extend and explore it more dynamically. That's not to say it's very interesting for someone to make a piece incorporating all kinds of styles. Anything goes by me if it works – if it achieves an integrity in what it sets out to do. If it doesn't, then it falls flat anyway.

Hybridizing with other art forms such as dance, sculpture, paint, film and computer is what I'm exploring particularly at the moment. I'm into the textuality of language and its plastic qualities: it can be squeezed, splashed, chopped and mixed; it can extend the aural by being chanted, have sound or music incorporated; it can extend the spatial by moving or creating its own dramatic space; it can be painted, sculpted, woven, built and smashed. You name it; it can.

I would be interested in working with other people jointly on the Web, but can't afford that yet, though *PQR* is soon set to go surfing. Its expense as that of multi-media equipment means that unless you can afford it, or are regularly attached to a University, then it is exclusive to wealthy users.

Hybridizing excites me, perhaps because of the way it can create a more whole physical experience as well as an intellectual and emotional one. It may also be because of my enjoyment of visual art too. Where work incorporates film and electronics, it is using the media of the millenium and moving forward, extending the communication of poetry rather than looking back to 'closed' structures and ideas. Hybridization is one of the ways it can be organic.

How do you select work for a poetry list/anthology? Should poetry lists/ anthologies demonstrate consistency or diversity?

Odyssey, which publishes collections and pamphlets, began by offering publication to people who came to the editor's (Derrick Woolf) attention through their submissions to the magazine of the same name. I believe that many small presses build up in this way. So initially, it was work which caught the editor's eye and included the offer of publication to some poets whom he heard read, as well as those which came in the post.

The restrictions come, for the small press as for the large, in balancing the books. If the press is run by someone who has the means and is prepared to subsidise it, or if it gets a regular grant, that's fine. It also helps if you are happy to continually be marketing, marketing. In our case the grant stopped, so we became more aware of the marketing potential of writers who will tout their own work. This does not necessarily go with the more exciting, innovative writers we like to promote. The grant is needed for promotion where a poet is not of a profile which makes his publication viable on its own. Ideally, Odyssey likes to support experimental writing as well as more interesting conventional work, but the reality is that, unless there is money and time (where one editor has a day job) to promote work, publication is not viable.

PQR publishes one double-page spread of one poet quarterly and, so far, has maintained alternate male and female poets equally. The editor has chosen to support his own 'list' poets and to invite others whose work he admires. The work has shown an eclectic range from conventional to innovative. This reflects the same range of reviews which the magazine gives space to. While keeping an eye on the larger presses and their lists, we like to give consideration to new small press poets and pamphlets, which may otherwise not get the coverage they deserve.

So we're diverse in the Odyssey and *PQR* publications, but some publishers have more specialist lists. It helps the writer to know if his work would suit that magazine or that list and it helps the reader to know he can generally trust a list or mag to suit his views. The diversity in *PQR* means, hopefully, that the divisions and camps are made aware of each other and even find value in each other, or are at least something to get dialogue going.

How do you address the lack of interest and understanding – states of animosity, even – that exist between working parts of the poetry world?

Definitions of kinds of poetry such as those outlined above can be useful until their supporters become antagonistic towards each other, when egos and attitudes say one is valid to the exclusion of others. This reputation has particularly been levelled at the 'Cambridge School', which for years had the reputation for being an exclusive clique. It is often levelled at Faber poets as being part of an often academic élite, who are believed to dismiss little presses as cranky or feeble.

For me, states of animosity whether in poetry or in the office are either laughable or pathetic, but reflect human nature, *not* the nature of poetry. They detract from the work and the idea.

I'm quite happy for you to hate someone's work, though I'd prefer you to have a substantial reason why, rather than denigrate the writer because of personal animosity.

This is highlighted for me as reviews editor of *PQR*. It could easily include (and to satisfy the vultures may soon include a 'Bile' column) strongly defamatory 'reviews', but I work from the standpoint that poetry sent for review deserves considered criticism. I don't find a useful place in reviews for personal slander. Unkind comments like 's/he writes crap' are only hurtful and don't lead to better writing, as they take the issue away from the work onto the personality. Go to the tabloids or the boxing ring to satisfy bullying. After all, if you feel someone's work is crap, you don't have to bother about it; don't read it. Considered criticism, however, might suggest a reason for your view and might help the emerging writer. Having said that, the wrangles that tangle some editorials and reviews in the small press provide plenty of interest and an edge, beside the quieter view *PQR* takes. There's room for both. In fact that's one of the healthy, exciting aspects of the Small Press.

The poet, if s/he deserves considered criticism, has to take the rough with the smooth in a review. If a poem does not work, or something jars a reviewer, then the poet should be made aware of this. How s/he responds to it – by modifications, serious explanation or paranoia – is his/her affair. It comes hardest to the writer (too often one who actually reads little poetry) who has a conceit that his poetry will shake the world and well, no, if you want to know, world-shattering poets are rare! Different poets hold different appeal for different groups of people anyway. Popular doesn't mean world-shattering either.

Probably holding on to and defending exclusive definitions of poetry reflects a human need for self-preservation and belief in our own importance or possessiveness, or a desire to claim our own territory. Attitude tells us more about the human nature of the poet or reviewer than it can about poetry.

I have learned that for every poem that leaves me cold there will be someone who rates it – even if I don't rate their opinion. So what? Go for what works for you.

What are your interests regarding questions of sexual politics and gender in poetry?

Because 'gender' became such a buzz-word and a hang-up especially around the universities and women's groups, the implication I feel is that, as a woman, I am *expected* to have a view. Well, I do, but I've not been a vociferous speaker about it. I thank those that have raised its profile for me, especially when I was an isolated writer at home in a conventional domestic situation, where looking after children took up creative energy for writing, time for going to readings or writers groups and money for subscribing to magazines. It need not be stifling if the family supports the importance of creativity. Men may argue that the same creative energy is sucked up by the day job. I don't disagree. With the existing Arts funding of poetry, poets of both sexes are faced with the battle between developing their work and existing financially. With a shift to men participating more fully in the family, they too may find it strains the creative energy, unless the partners agree on giving space to writing.

On my personal level, this space was not negotiated successfully. It meant my poetic sensibility was not nurtured well and was fed by the library and the High Street bookshops with predominantly male-edited and male-filled shelves. Even the legendary *Children of Albion*, edited by Michael Horovitz, included only five women among sixty three or so men and the standard bearer *Oxford Book of Twentieth Century English Verse*, chosen by Philip Larkin, contained just over twenty women among over two hundred poets. Except for anthologies of women poets, the ratios nowadays are still heavily weighted towards men. Of thirty-six poets under the critical scrutiny of Sean O'Brien in *The De-Regulated Muse*, seven are female. There are two women in Faber's current list for poetry. Bloodaxe gives credible space to women poets, yet at a rough count of their current list, it shows a bias of over 150 men to about 83 women.

In Summer 1994 *Odyssey* Magazine carried in its listings the ratios of men to women appearing in current issues of various magazines: *Envoi* 60:40, *Spectrum* 64:36, *Smith's Knoll* 75:25, *Fatchance* (with women editors) 63:37, *Scratch* 68:32, *Ramraid Extraordinaire* 87:13, *Angel Exhaust* 86:14, *Terrible*

Work 84:16, *Iron* 63:37, *Headlock* 68:32. Only *The Rialto* from the bunch listed showed some parity between the sexes with 48:52.

How is it if I dip in our current listings box? At a rough count not much better. My quick count may be one or two out, but it appears *The Rialto* is still fairly even with 23:18. *Poetry London Newsletter* shows a balance in the women's favour of 7:9 in one issue and 10:14 in another. *Smith's Knoll* is much improved with 25:23, but many others show at a rough count a strong male bias as follows: *The North* 20:7, *Angel Exhaust* 20:3, *Blade* 18:3, *Envoi* 51:18, *Affectionate Punch* 26:8.

So the phallocentric society for whatever reasons still prevails in poetry publishing – I know of next to no senior women editors in the major poetry publishing houses – though several small presses and women's presses are redressing the balance.

For me, some of the most exciting and daring poetry I come across is by women, but I have to go in search of them. They suffer the double bind of being less well profiled, because of both the female imbalance and the lack of exposure of experimental work.

What is the point of an anthology?

The whole activity of poetry is too amorphous and interwoven to have rigidly defined boundaries, but an anthology can give us a handle on and a connecting thread between poets. It is this handle, or way in, that I see as valuable, or 'the point' as you put it, of anthologies. Ideally they will extend the reader's knowledge, be it introducing the new reader to poetry *per se*, or introducing the habitual reader to a new angle or range of work. Particularly with innovative work it helps to raise the profile of the avant garde.

There is the drawback of a writer becoming known by their anthologised poems and little else, though I haven't yet seen an anthology of the most anthologised poems!

The question of increased sales for anthologies as opposed to individual collections does not have to be derogatory – implying greed by the publisher. Increased sales of poetry can surely be useful in keeping the somewhat flickering candle of poetry burning among the Olympic flames of the best-sellers. Also the revenue from increased sales can/should go towards subsidising less lucrative individual collections. Thirdly, appearing in an anthology can inform readers who can then go and seek out individual collections. Fourthly, appearing in an anthology, from the poet's point of view can present his or her work to a wider audience than may already know it. It's not all bad; in fact, it looks generally positive.

Why still publish books in the 'electronic age'?

With the advent of electricity, candles did not become obsolete; their use changed. With the advent of plastic, china and wood did not cease to be used. So I don't see that books will necessarily become obsolete. They will have more variety available so that they may be read between conventional covers, or on your palm-top, or heard on CDs, cassettes and whatever supersedes them, as well as being seen on the big screen.

Though I enjoy these, I'm not alone in also enjoying the physical handling of a book – its touch, its colour and texture, the way it feels and even its smell, its portability, putting it in your pocket, making marginalia, its ease of access and the atmosphere it creates when ranged around a room in shelves or abandoned on the coffee table.

At the moment it is still a cheaper way of reading for those of us who cannot afford to get on-line. We may have free libraries, but that doesn't yet include free access to the Internet. And we can refer to a book, flicking from page to page at once, instead of having to wait for it to be down-loaded and then only being able to refer to one page at a time.

Also, it's altogether more conducive to reading in the bath or in bed! Added to which, there is the instinct of ownership; its a favourite collectable and how do you own/collect books you refer to on the Web except by downloading them and printing them into book-form?

Long live the book!

Richard Caddel

'Making the Words Dance'

Prolific input, low output. Sometimes I can't understand how I ever got to put two words together. I write most days, and of course most of it gets crossed out, or doesn't immediately do what it's meant to do, but I still think that practice element is important: when things do start to cohere, I'm ready. It's not a methodology they'd teach you at the job centre, and I'm not particularly proud of it, but I don't see any alternative – for me. I went to school with Objectivist method, learning to pare and shape, and that's never left me. So that notes get scribbled into the current notebook – odd phrases, words – which later get drawn into projects of one kind or another, and thence into drafts which I can work with over a period of time. There might be five or six proto-projects in drafts at any one time. Loss-of-notebook (which happened last year) is therefore a nightmare accident which it takes ages to recover from. Some of the on-going current interests include borders (we all live on them), Old Welsh poetry (still), and (in the broadest sense) environment – but these change. These days also I'm more consciously wanting the sound of the piece to be revealed to me, to hear the beats and patterning in the language forming a whole, so I keep working until this happens. I'm making scores, which can be realised in a number of ways – by me, or, I hope, by anyone. Each job has its own requirements, and I've tackled quite a range over the last thirty years – difficult therefore for me to generalise about my work as a whole.

My work is rooted in the linguistic muck of the life around it – words of family and friends are pirated freely, and so are the books I read and work with. Rhythms of my daily routines are in there from the first (my early work has the subsound of the train which carried me to and from work; these days there's a stronger walking rhythm). My social and political stance is implicit throughout the work, I'd say: it sits alongside the personal and domestic, because the domestic is political too. Since much of my working day up to now has been spent deep in concerns of the job (library) the act of writing has become – at times – squeezed, and it's been pointed out to me that my syntax is increasingly fragmentary. Well, so's my life, and so too is the life of most of my readers. I'm not constructing some kind of platonic dream world here, I'm more interested in the one we share *now*. At present I'm having to contemplate – in the future at some point – an earlyish health-related retirement from library grind: that will alter drastically the logistics of my writing.

I envy prolific writers in some sense, but can't emulate them. There's part of me which needs as much brevity as possible – 'save the time of the reader' is one of the laws of library science, and that's a spirit I think poets would do well to adopt. No surprise, then to find that many of the writers of past or present who I have most time for (would walk miles uphill in the rain to find new work by) are those for whom grace and precision are evident virtues. Bunting, Niedecker and the Objectivists. Creeley. Contemporaries such as Tony Baker, John Seed, Harriet Tarlo (for instance). A wider circle with such as Raworth, Harwood, Roy Fisher. But this list could be endless, and – thank heavens! – would in no way be limited to those with whom I share concerns. I'm picking up what I want from *all* the writers I read.

Writing pre-dated editorial activity for me, by only a short while. When I began to write, friends around me were doing the same sort of thing: I was shocked to find that although they recognised the difficulties we'd all have in presenting our work, they weren't prepared to do a thing about it except moan. It seemed to me logical to expect to be involved in editing, publishing and readings organising as well – just as it's logical to do a bit towards the preparation and washing up of a meal. Also, it was an extension of my reading and performing practice, to want to *realise* texts which I admired. Ann and I started Pig Press to present work by friends, in the first place, and then increasingly the work of writers I'd become interested in.

I was trained as a musician. Quite often the way I pick up on a writer is by hearing him/her read (organising readings has been another of my editorial activities) or by sounding them myself. As I've said, the sound shape of a work is increasingly the bit by which it stands or falls, as far as I'm concerned, and when I stop getting a thrill off the sound of language, well, I hope I have the guts to retire gracefully. Equally, some writers have disappointed me so systematically by their lack of concern for the text as sound that I've never been able to have a good word for them. The reader who turned up and prefaced his boring reading with 'well, I think my poems are better read in silence, on the page' – I've never forgiven him for wasting all our time for his measly fee, and I've never wasted any more of my own time on his ear-dead work. Poetry is, of itself, a 'hybrid' then (for me) – it exists on the page, waiting to become music, and equally, on the page, it has visual impact and meaning: I want both.

I've collaborated with visual artists in one sense or another, but never satisfactorily – artists always seem to shrink from meddling with my texts, and to get all bristly when I want to scribble on their images. Yet without such hands-on collaboration, the projects become – for me – just illustration: here's a thought, let's stick a tail on it. Musicians, sadly, seem to back off from working with me – presumably wary again of me wanting to muck around with their scores... Yet when I worked with Lee Harwood on *Wine Tales* we got along quite merrily, though we're very different people – altered each others' writing (by negotiation – we're both Union men) and came up with a unified work which neither of us could've written alone.

As an editor, my primary act of faith is to the writers I edit. Organising a reading, I want the reader to perform as they'd wish. Publishing a book, I want it to look as the author wants it. A good editor is (practically) invisible. One publisher I've spoken to has prided himself on his ability to squeeze such a wide range of poets into his 'house style'. That seems a complete travesty to me, and the various printers of Pig Press books have had nightmares dealing with the small-but-significant elements of design which have made every book different. The dictates of the text must come first. As an editor of anthologies, the task is slightly different: you can't expect the magazine or publisher to respect such a range of authorial demand, so some compromise is needed. Nevertheless, in preparing *Other* for publication, we took some pains to explain to a hard-pressed design and typography department some of the widely varying orthographies of 'our' poets – and they responded well. I'm less than interested in 'lists' – fantasy poetic football teams – and if you put all the Pig Press or *Other* authors together in one room you'd have a huge fight on your hands in no time. No canons: canons close options.

Some of the most heart-stopping moments in poetry often appear simple: invariably, when you consider them closely, they're anything but simple... A lot of the work from Pig Press – and in *Other*, or in the magazine issues I've been involved in – and in the readings I've promoted – could be classed as 'difficult' to some critical backgrounds. I'd maintain that it has difficult elements in it, perhaps – but that most difficulties are made by readers or critics who bring their own predetermined expectations to the work, and aren't prepared to make some effort themselves. I'm sorry if this sounds tough: it's been my experience that most worthwhile things in life do involve an element of difficulty. I'm damned if I'll kowtow to the general tellytubby consumer culture we have pressed on us which suggests that if you have to chew it, it ain't food. Louis Zukofsky (ok – he's difficult – but well worth it!) quoted Einstein to the effect that 'everything in the Universe should be as simple as it can be – *but not simpler*'. I once had a rejection note from a publisher describing my work as 'awkward and difficult' and in some ways I'm happy with that! Anyway, I think most of the supposed difficulties in poetry are caused by people who just aren't used to listening. 'Stand up and use your ears, like a man' quoth Charles Ives to one of his critics.

The same Zukofsky said, uncompromisingly, that 'poetry is for interested people' – interested, that is, not just in poetry, but in the *matter* of poetry, which is as broad as the world. The number of people who can cope with this may be small – certainly less than the numbers flocking to the latest beach novel – but they are there, and they do, consistently, need feeding. Poetry publishers might take heart in the fact that, the more varied a diet they present, the more units they move. In sales terms (*pace* Heaney) compared with global population figures, and blockbuster novels, there's not actually much difference between the turn around of an 'easy' anecdotal 'mainstream' poet with lotsa hype, and a wild and whacky one from an unknown stable – it just feels that way on the ground. I speak, of course, of living poets – everyone knows that dead poets sell more... Let's be frank, if you wanted stardom, you should've been a TV chef.

Of course there are many divisions in 'contemporary poetry', and 'binary myths' isn't the half of it. None of them allow me to stop reading and responding across as wide a range as I can, listening, I hope, to work across the spectrum. I do it because I enjoy it – but it's a lonely job at times. What annoys me, perpetually, is the snottiness of mainstream poetry supporters towards poetries which don't make it into the sanctified organs of culture – the idea that there's some unified cultural yardstick which can measure poetry, and include the worthy and exclude the unworthy. I'm tired of the condescension which writers like (say) Lee Harwood, or Harry Guest or Gael Turnbull get treated with – writers with unique and honourable outputs over many years, which should earn them respect – and yet, as I write, none of these major figures has a Collected or Selected in print. Shame on you, so-called Big Presses. As I've said, ear-dead anecdotal poetry bores me stiff, so I'd be wasting my time publishing or promoting it (though I keep probing it, just in case) – besides, others from the mainstream seem to be falling over themselves to do so. On the other hand, there's a real need for more presses which cover a range of poetries, or which publish across the barricades. I freely admit that Pig Press didn't go far in that direction, though in the poetry readings I've organised I've generally tried to make a mix and got precious little in the way of thanks for it – poets are generally a prickly bunch.

When Peter Quartermain and I were editing *Other*, I got frequent bouts of conscience: was it right to publish such an obviously partisan anthology? Shouldn't I be trying the reach-out-hands routine one more time? Well, the answer came in the little spate of *fin-de-siecle* 'survey' anthologies of British poetry since the war, such as Armitage 'n' Crawford, and O'Brien (two spookily similar products – 'Dolly the Anthology' as one commentator dubbed them). Obviously, there's good work in both – but sadly it's also true that whole layers of achievement have been quite simply ignored – not referred to and dismissed, simply treated as if they didn't exist. What arrogance, from editors assuming the role of surveyors! What sheer unmitigated disrespect to the serious and sustained work of whole generations of writers! In that context, our necessary *Other* (which acknowledges the presence and activities of writers not included, and makes no shallow claims to 'survey') seems to me to be a justified and timely corrective to another bout of mainstream off-handedness. In that context too I understand perfectly the drive to prepare 'separatist' anthologies of, say, women's poetry, and have welcomed many of the productions: *Out Of Everywhere* has been, for me, one of the finest anthologies of recent years. You ask, curiously, 'has poetry publishing become a male preserve?' Historically, surely, poetry has *almost exclusively* been a male preserve (Wavell's classic anthology *Other Men's Flowers* is aptly titled...) – happily, and significantly, this boy's club is breaking down a bit (not enough, and not fast enough, perhaps). Interesting to note that this is achieved, in many cases, not by putting women into the temples of male culture, but by bypassing such edifices altogether. And you don't need a PhD to see that some of the most exciting innovative writing around at present is coming from women.

Anthologies are prepared by professed experts, and criticised and taught by professed experts. There's a real danger that we all forget that the prime and most obvious value of an anthology is to introduce work to a non-expert. At an early point in my life I came across, in close succession: (a) Alvarez's *The New Poetry* and (b) Horovitz's *Children of Albion* – both important anthologies from which I've benefited immensely. It struck me then that with these two I had a map for further exploration, which didn't rob me of choice, but which opened up immense possibilities. Obviously, there were angels and turkeys in both, and for myself, I found one set more alluring than the other in terms of my own development – but that's not the point: I can thank those anthologists for presenting me with the initial maps. I know that people read *The New British Poetry* (Paladin 1988) and that it stayed with them – bizarrely, I've had contact from several people (ok, not hundreds) who read my work there, and wanted to say something about it: that's a great feeling for me. This suggests to me that there's a sense in which depriving a poet or group of poets of anthology space is damaging to their readership. It may not matter greatly – and indeed some writers have positively relished the freedom of obscurity in which they've developed – but there it is. The motivation behind *Other* was not to create a new canonical in-crowd, but to make a rough map to point a US academic readership towards work which would otherwise be hidden from them. It's self-evidently not comprehensive, but it goes some way. In our introduction we quote the wonderful Maurice Scully's statement that there is 'a completely buried 'modernist/experimental' tradition'. If it goes a few spadefuls towards revealing this tradition, it will have been worthwhile.

Social and political motivation... I am socially and politically motivated, and I hope that's evident in my poetry. But as a rule, if I want to make a straight social/political statement, I don't use poetry.

It should be clear by now that I'm committed to the sound of language, and to the production of scores for that purpose, and the curation of performances. It's a full time job, and though I expect other media to continue to develop, I stick – on the whole – with books. People have trumpeted the death of the book for donkey's years, and there it is still, handy, pocketable, hospitable. I read John Tranter's webzine *Jacket* regularly, it's great – and I use e-mail too. I set up the 'British and Irish Poets List' in 1996 to facilitate discussion amongst the more innovative practitioners. It's an open list (I think that's important) so not all the exchanges are of earth-shattering brilliance or insight, and at times it gets a bit heated. But already, I think, it's brought together – uneasily at times – writers of widely differing backgrounds, into a keenly felt but (moderately) amicable dialogue. There are other lists for poets, but life's short, and running this one takes time – so I rely on friends to deal me into the core dialogue on other lists.

Poetry – the sound, the crunch of language, and the dance of vowels and consonants – is a great continuing adventure for me: if I pass any of that along to others in my own writing, or in my editing, well, it's been worthwhile.

Ken Edwards

Is contemporary poetry a divided thing? Divided which ways? How are you bridging the gaps?

The assumption behind this question may be that healing the breach in contemporary poetry is an admirable goal, and that this is the task of editor-writers. I would challenge such an assumption. There may be very good reasons why poetry is divided. After all, so are other art forms. Nobody is too bothered that 'music' doesn't form a coherent category. You wouldn't programme a concert in which the string quartets of James Dillon alternated with the Spice Girls performing their recent hits (no disrespect to either). Boundary blur, and its potential for breaking into a new unknown, is one thing; but a too-eager rush towards fusion results either in blandness or ludicrous category error.

More of a problem is the *denial* of categories or paradigms in poetry. Thus, any poetry not pursuing the goals and norms of creative writing classes at their worst, or of the book reviewers in the Sunday papers ('clarity of expression', 'communication with the reader', 'arresting metaphor', 'epiphany', and all that palaver) risks being perceived either as inferior or incomprehensible. (Example: a literary funding apparatchik, later Faber poet, advises me in 1995 that one of the selling points of the proposed Reality Street anthology *Out of Everywhere* is that it gives encouragement to young women poets who haven't the skills to write in normative ways.)

The British poetry 'avant-garde' (for want of a better term – and I haven't found a better term, since I started researching this area for a belated, part-time PhD) is sometimes characterised as divided between the 'Cambridge' and 'London' tendencies. Many deny this division. If it does exist, then that is something I *would* like to bridge, both as a writer and editor. But I'm not generally in the business of infill.

Do we need anthologies which divide poets thematically / stylistically / politically / gender-wise?

While on the subject of anthologies – and *Out of Everywhere* in particular – I was annoyed by a review that suggested the only thing the contributors had in common was their gender. This was emphatically *not* the project devised by Maggie O'Sullivan and myself. (That's not to say there aren't important stylistic differences between the contributors, of course.) It was an attempt to chart a recent phenomenon – the feminisation of 'experimental' writing. It's very noticeable that the 'language-centred' writing movement in the US, once heavily male-dominated, has thrown up more and more women in the past ten years. This process lags behind a little in this country, but is also starting to happen here.

In fact, I wouldn't mind seeing a follow-up anthology in which some male participants were included. Could really set the cat among the pigeons.

In the end, anthologies are just shop-windows, if you'll excuse the commercial terminology. Maybe reference resources would be a better term. The afterword to *Out Of Everywhere* encourages readers, having browsed, to follow up any interests that have been awakened by seeking out individual collections by the poets.

I have participated in the editing of two anthologies now, and have sworn each time never to get involved in another. It's a sweat, and an irritant. But I'm glad I did them. The first was *The New British Poetry* published by Paladin in 1988. That was criticised for dividing up the 80-odd contributors into four discrete sections, the other three being edited by Fred D'Aguiar (Black British poets), Gillian Allnutt ('quote feminist unquote') and Eric Mottram. The alternative would have been to mix the four selections together, in alphabetical order or whatever. However, I felt the way we did it, with all its drawbacks, was the honest way. The sections did form coherent and self-contained communities of poets – although my and Eric's sections could have been run together. Of course, group formation has its obvious perils.

Do we need such selections? They are like Wittgenstein's ladder, to be discarded after use.

How does your writing inform your work as an editor?

I started writing 'seriously' (that is, being serious about the possibility of others reading it) in the early/mid-1970s – in my early/mid-20s. Though I had written poetry of stunning pretentiousness and mediocrity before, it was as a fiction writer that I wanted to make my mark. I had some success, with short stories being published in the *Transatlantic Review*, *Bananas* and the Arts Council anthology *New Stories 2*. I remember Ian McEwan was a highly touted short story writer at the time, getting into the magazines I had been eyeing next. He's about two years older than me. However, I never could get very excited about his writing. My models were Kafka, Beckett, Donald Barthelme, Thomas Pynchon, the science-fiction writers of *New Worlds* magazine.

After my story was in *New Stories 2*, Derwent May, editor at Chatto & Windus, asked me if I was working on a novel and, if so, to send it to him. I *was* working on one, but I couldn't see a way of translating the highly charged prose and discontinuous narrative techniques I had been developing into the longer form of the novel. I did complete a novel eventually, but was profoundly disillusioned with it almost as soon as I'd finished. So I stopped writing fiction.

About this time – 1975 onwards – I started getting interested in poetry again. I was involved in a poetry workshop with Robert Hampson and Peter Barry – we were reading Roy Fisher, Charles Olson, Tristan Tzara: surrealism, open-field techniques, the open text. I started going to events at the Poetry Society, which was really buzzing then with all sorts of experimenting – that all came to an end in 1977, when the Arts Council intervened and most of the poets who had been on the ruling council resigned in protest. I got to know poets like David Miller, Paul Brown, Mike Dobbie, Allen Fisher, many of whom were also involved in small press publishing, because the big publishers were not interested in any writing that was at all challenging, as far as I could see. *Poetry Information* magazine was a great source of data and inspiration. It was an exciting time.

Are these same big publishers still uninterested in challenging writing?
I think the situation now is worse, if anything – the accountants are in charge!

Robert, Peter and I had edited a magazine called *Alembic*, at first as a showcase for our own poetry and then to publish other contemporary poetry that interested us. From 1978, initially as an offshoot of this, I started a magazine called *Reality Studios*. The name was taken from a Burroughs quote – 'storm the reality studios and re-take the universe' – later used by the Situationists. The first few issues were duplicated on my own Roneo, in tiny runs. In 1975 and 1976 I had made contact with James Sherry in New York, and, through him, the group of poets and writers centred round $L=A=N=G=U=A=G=E$ magazine: so *Reality Studios* became the first British magazine to publish the work of Charles Bernstein, Bruce Andrews, Bob Perelman, Alan Davies, Rae Armantrout, Steve Benson, Diane Ward, Larry Price, as well as British poets such as Allen Fisher, Douglas Oliver, Peter Riley, Wendy Mulford, Maggie O'Sullivan, Bob Cobbing, Glenda George, Alan Halsey, Lee Harwood, John Wilkinson. I also was keen to include book reviews and theoretical writing. I was impressed with the way the Americans *thought* about their work and were willing to share those thoughts and argue in public, rather than retreating into little cliques, as seemed to be the tendency here.

Is this still a tendency?
Sadly, yes – though I think internet discussion lists such as British-Poets have helped open things out a little.

Reality Studios lasted ten years. It was a learning process for me, and a way of making contact with other writers. I'm proud of what I did with that magazine.

But eventually, it became a burden, as magazine editing tends to, particularly as there was very little funding support.

During that period, I wrote no fiction, but had several books and chapbooks of poetry out, all published by other small presses. I had a policy of not self-publishing my poetry. Nothing against people who do so, it was just my decision. In the early 1980s Galloping Dog Press, run by Peter Hodgkiss, who used to edit *Poetry Information*, published *Tilth* and *Drumming & Poems*, the latter of which I regard as a breakthrough in my work, bringing together linguistic, musical and political concerns. Ric Caddel's Pig Press published my 1986 book *Intensive Care*, which is a book I still regard highly, though it's very dark in outlook, coming at a time of political pessimism. All these books are now out of print. In 1992 James Sherry's New York press Roof Books published *Good Science*, and in 1993 Ian Robinson published *3,600 Weekends* under the Oasis Books imprint. I have never attempted to submit my work to the Fabers and OUPs, as I imagine it would be a waste of time.

As an editor and publisher, my aim is to publish exactly what I would like to read myself but is not being catered for by the big publishers. This has nothing to do with 'gaps in the market' – I have never been sales-led, though it's nice to have a relatively good seller such as *Out of Everywhere*, which is on the way to selling 1,500 copies, by far the biggest edition I've ever been involved with.

That book is part of my current publishing venture, Reality Street Editions. This began in 1993, when Reality Studios, which still existed as an imprint although the magazine had stopped, merged with Street Editions, Wendy Mulford's press. I suppose it was an attempt to unite two traditions from left-field in the poetry scene. Street Editions had published mostly Cambridge-based poets during the 1970s, at first mainly men, but latterly with an increasing interest in the modernist/feminist nexus. Wendy and I have been close friends since we met in 1987 – actually on the Holywell to Dun Laogheare ferry on the way to a poetry festival organised in Dublin by Maurice Scully. Wendy withdrew from active participation in Reality Street in 1997, but the press goes on and I'm trying to keep alive the tradition she started with Street Editions. At the time of writing this we have published 16 titles.

In the early 1990s I returned to fiction writing after a period when I rejected it. I seemed suddenly to find a way of turning to narrative ends the language procedures I had been experimenting with. I wrote most of my novel *Futures* during a six-week stay at Hawthornden Castle writers' retreat near Edinburgh in 1990. I hawked it around publishers and eventually a small press called Barrington Books, based in Preston, who had published Nicholas Royle's first novel, agreed to take it on. But after a year of hanging about, they went out of business. So eventually, I decided to publish it under the Reality Street imprint in 1998, breaking my 'no self-publishing' rule. I'm pleased I did. Most fiction published in this country today bores me, but I would like Reality Street to get into the radical/experimental end of this area. However, it requires more resources than I can muster at present.

I came to be an editor and publisher, almost by necessity, as a result of the kind of writing I have been doing, which is regarded as profoundly uncommercial. But the fact is, I don't know if or how my writing has informed my work as an editor. It might be more pertinent to pose the opposite question: how has my editing influenced me as a writer? It has exposed me to a variety of modes and techniques, and kept me in touch with a community of writers and poets. If I abandoned the small press work, as I've sometimes contemplated, it would give me a lot more time for my writing, but perhaps to its detriment. I think all writers need that contact with other writers to keep them recharged, and publishing has given me that.

What important influences have shaped your current interests? What are you reading at present?

After a period during which I thought the British avant-garde had had its day in the 1970s and 80s, I'm glad to say there is a new wave now of younger poets bringing with them the injection of energy we need every now and then: writing energy, publishing and entrepreneurial energy. I go regularly to the SubVoicive reading series in London, which has gone through periodic lulls but is currently putting on some very strong readings under Lawrence Upton's direction. I've enjoyed recent readings by younger poets such as Ira Lightman, Rob Holloway, Keston Sutherland, Rob MacKenzie, Karlien van den Beukel and Dell Olson, to name a few. Not to mention yourself, Andy! And by older stagers such as Anne Waldman, Anselm Hollo, Bob Perelman, Robert Sheppard, John Wilkinson. Miles Champion is a terrific poet and a tireless organiser – the readings he's involved with in Spitalfields in East London are consistently interesting. A soundless reading by Tertia Longmire and the deaf poet Aaron Williamson was recently memorable.

My own poetry is going in different directions: more abstract in some of my musical collaborations; more lyrical elsewhere. I'm severely distorting the sonnet in a series of poems with the working title *Eight Plus Six*. I take as my reference points everyone from Sir Thomas Wyatt to Bernadette Mayer. Another important direction is towards prose – both shorter prose, which has always been an element in the mix of such books as *Drumming* or *Intensive Care*, and longer, narrative prose. I have two novels on the go. I am constantly disappointed by contemporary novels. I've recently re-read *Tristram Shandy* for the first time since my teens – it's more contemporary than anything I've read this year. Pynchon's *Mason & Dixon* parodies the 18th century style brilliantly, but the conceit gets tedious eventually. I'm currently reading Richard Powers' *Galatea 2.2*, in which I'm interested in the ideas about artificial intelligence, but I find it very mannered. What else? Steven Mithen's *The Prehistory of the Mind*. As for poetry: Maurice Scully's *Steps*, Jennifer Moxley's *Imagination Verses* and most recently the transatlantic collaboration between Alan Halsey and Karen Mac Cormack, *Fit to Print*.

Are you interested in hybridizing poetries, or hybridizing poetry with other art forms? Have you collaborated with other artists or writers recently?

I'm working with musicians and have been composing music and getting more interested in the text/music interface. *Bruised Rationals*, a piece of mine combining spoken text with written and improvised music for a large ensemble, has been performed several times by the London COMA Ensemble, a group of amateur musicians with whom I play violin. At the time of writing this, I'm rehearsing duos with my friend Elaine Randle, who plays flute, keyboards and percussion. Also co-writing an opera with four others: Janet Davey, Alan Taylor, Rebekka Wedell and Ann Wolff. We're still working on the libretto.

As far as the press goes, we've published one book/CD package (cris cheek & Sianed Jones's *Songs from Navigation*) and I'd love to do more hybrid book/audio publishing of this kind if the resources are available.

I'm listening to Birtwistle (*The Mask of Orpheus*), Berio, Xenakis, Francesconi, Stravinsky, Bach, Monteverdi, John Coltrane, Anthony Braxton, the Rova quartet, Khaled, Neneh Cherry, flamenco, Cuban music.

Are you interested in electronic publishing? Which e-journals, discussion lists & poetry websites do you use?

John Cayley has helped me develop the Reality Street website. So far, it's basically an electronic version of the catalogue – one of these days, I'll get down to developing it with extracts from published and forthcoming books. I'm not totally convinced yet about electronic publishing. John's own kinetic poetry beautifully exploits the electronic medium, but very few others are doing comparable work of any interest. I hate reading conventional poetry or prose on screen because I can't relax with it – I'd rather print it and read off the hard copy, but that seems like re-inventing the book in a rather cumbersome way. I rarely visit other websites. One day we'll probably be reading our own personal screens, but at present the technology is not nearly transparent or cheap enough, and aesthetically unpleasing. There is no evidence that books are dying, rather the reverse – there's an explosion of print publishing, partly because the technology – DTP typesetting/design and short-run litho printing – has become much cheaper in the past decade.

I have subscribed to the Poetics discussion list, run from Buffalo, USA, for some years, but currently I'm off-line as I can't cope with reading the volume of e-mail it generates. I also subscribe to the British-Poets list, which is a good forum for discussion about innovative poetry, when it doesn't descend into personal grumbles and backbiting. E-mail has definitely transformed national and international communications.

Peter Finch

What's going on in contemporary poetry that interests you? Is poetry in a healthy state at the moment or is it heading nowhere?

I'm pretty interested in the whole of the British New Poetries (or whatever we want to call it). The approaches adopted years back by poets such as Allen Fisher, Bill Griffiths, Thomas A Clark and especially Tom Raworth continues to fascinate me and I am much enthused by the large number of writers who, over the years, have now joined them and still continue to join. Allen Fisher in particular is a giant among UK writers who somehow manages to stay outside of the usual lit. crit trap, has not got himself bogged down in the reading circuit and still appears as fresh a voice today as he did in the early seventies. His work is large scale involving multi-volume projects and is informed to a significant extent by the worlds of visual art and science. He is one of the UK's unsung best. Add to this the post-LANGUAGE work that flows in across the water from the US and we have a pretty healthy-seeming backdrop. Writers do not appear afraid to push at the boundaries now. There was a time when I looked to Europe but I guess that time is over. Major contemporary significances for me are now English, Scottish, Irish or American.

At base, though, there is a problem and that's the sheer diversity of poetry itself. Outside the aforementioned areas of personal interest lie most of what the critics, the Universities, the amateur poetry dabblers and the public consumers (such as they are) perceive as the real stuff. The UK New gen extended, the English traditional, the minority Caribbean black, the academic backwaters, the stage performances, the slam shouters, the Welsh, Irish and Scottish ethnicities. And there is stuff here too that really interests me. But the enormous range of it all gives us poetry as scatter gun. No focus, no agreed direction, no single handle to hold onto. Everything there ever was repeated and done so simultaneously. I am here too, taking advantage of my modernist upbringing; finding what I've been doing for the past thirty years is fashionable again; watching others hijack old ideas and retread them as if they were new and as if they were their own. This is what post-modernism teaches us is the way on.

What chances and risks are taken in your own work, or the work you have edited/ published?

Chances imply risk of creative failure or risk of misunderstanding. The misunderstanding part has never bothered me. Some poets start with the idea of the reader in mind – if the work cannot cross to other ears or eyes then it is doomed. Others play to the lowest common denominator, that is they make everything they do accessible and instant. Like an issue of *Bella* or *Best* or a tv soap. I've had brushes with this approach when I've been up there on stage performing and getting that buzz you get from instant audience reaction. It makes you lean towards the neat ending, the joke, the instant effect. If they don't understand you then you are lost. And I've done that. Gone out and worked on pieces to work in just that kind of situation. A slab of my work from the early 80s was defined by its ability to succeed when read at 2.00 am to drunken students at a Monday night jazz club. There was no band – too expensive – they used poets instead. Props helped – a loud hailer, explosions, the whirled tube from the back of the tumble dryer. When the students wouldn't listen I stood next to them and put the amplified cone to their ears. If the poem didn't succeed under those conditions then I abandoned it. But I've returned again now to the idea that audiences themselves have to do some of the work (and in some cases quite a lot of the work). So they do not get every reference contained in the poem. So it sounds random or fragmented or self-indulgent. So what. Poetry is not always mathematics. Poetry is not geometric shape. There are no hard rules and ultimate forms. The reader participates as much as the writer.

Much of the material I included in the 21 issue run of my magazine *second aeon*, which was published between 1966 and 1974, ran extreme risks. It was the risk that excited me. If I could get our literary guardians hopping up and down by the newness or the unadulterated wildness of what I published then so much the better. Bob Cobbing taught me a lot here – and I owe him a huge debt. If it's good put it out. Do it fast. Push the boundary and push the form. He relished bad publicity and drew strength from the fact that the average poetry reading attendee appeared utterly baffled by what he did. The audience needed to be stretched. The poet was not there simply to entertain. And by this he did not mean sloppy creative indulgence. The poets had to turn creative somersaults in order to achieve anything at all.

Unfortunately publishing difficult and inaccessible material does not lead to huge sales. Concrete, sound and other experimental, alternative poetry sold in dozens rather than hundreds of copies. The choice for the publisher was to either stay totally in the field and become an obscure specialist, or to add it to the mix and go for global coverage. I chose the latter route and mixed the new in with the rest and by dint of good marketing, fair judgement and a slab of street-cred managed to reach pretty high little mag sales. I gained an acceptance among seekers of the real and hunters for the new. Libraries everywhere subscribed, bookshop sales across the UK were responsive. Among the poetry community *second aeon* became an arbiter of taste and a place to be seen and the Americans loved what I did, yet I was never once in my entire career as a publisher mentioned by any national newspaper. Had I been based in London rather than what was then perceived as the non-metropolitan sticks then I am sure things would have been different. When *Poetry Review* ran aground I was actually offered the editorship but because of a career move (I was busy establishing the Oriel Bookshop) turned it down. Maybe I should have accepted. So it goes.

How does your writing inform your work as an editor?

It was actually always the other way around. The more you read the wider your creative edge. The more you do then the more you do. I came into contact with a huge range of poets, their new work and their published material. Editors get immersed like this constantly. And when you surface you either do something else altogether or you spark off work of your own. The latter was me.

Coming back to Cardiff from one of my many trips to London, the Poetry Society in the Nuttall/MacSweeney/Mottram years, Poets Conference, the Association of Little Presses' bookfairs, the gatherings of Cobbing, Bill Griffiths, Peter Mayer, Henri Chopin, Andrew Lloyd, and others always set me at it furiously writing.

What processes lie behind the writing of your poems? Are you prolific?

Prolific in bursts. Then long stretches of silence. That's the way it is now. The time factor is very important. My present job (running the Welsh National Literature Promotion Agency – Academi) takes up all my time and gets all my energy. There is very little of either left over for my own creativity. But that's at present. Things will change again, they always do. I wrote *make*, one of my best, published by Peter Hodgkiss's Galloping Dog Press in 1990, during one of the periodic lulls in my job as bookshop manager at Oriel. At times trade would drop, external demand from the owners (The Welsh Arts Council) would be elsewhere (i.e. they would be engaged in some new project and not at it poking me into new action) and I'd have a decent and competent staff behind me to carry out the daily tasks. Difficulties would recede. *make* was largely composed sitting in my first floor office watching the slow movement of the city from the window. The book is full of literary and bookselling references drawn from the stock passing through my hands and mixed in with observations of passers by, callers and the building site over the road. I'd recently read a compendium from that creative genius, Jackson Mac Low, and was interested in seeing how far I could push the verbal fragment.

On other occasions different forces have been applied. *The Cheng Man Ch'ing Variations* were written as a long process piece, taking the idea of body movement and spiritual progress as exemplified by Cheng Man Ch'ing and pushing these through a series of variations. I was deep into Tai Chi at the time and Man Ching was the acknowledged Chinese master of the Yang form. The philosophy behind the art and at the heart of Taoism informed the piece. I was careful not to publish any reference to tai chi in the first edition of the work (Writers Forum) and it was interesting to see how many readers managed to reach totally unexpected conclusions without this small clue. Cheng Man Ch'ing was seen as an opium driven waster, a Chinese restaurant owner, a fictional alternative persona, a character from Eastern literature and as a local acquaintance. In reality he was none of these things. At the time of the construction of this piece I was also looking at ways in which the photocopier could distort reality and simultaneously mimic street poster vandalism and the weathering of printed material. Mid 80s council estate reality. I took a photographic image of Cheng Man Ch'ing and processed it in ways similar to those I was using for the text of the piece. 'So where do you get your inspiration' someone asked me at the time. 'Does it come from life?' It does and then again it does not. Pretty Zen.

How often do you write?

I try to protect at least one day a week where I have the phone off hook and the doorbell unbattered. I ask repair men not to call at this time. The space is precious and very hard fought for. Any old time will not do. I need an early start and really have to avoid speaking to anyone. People do not understand this, even those close to me. Nonetheless, if I am to write anything at all then the selfish removal of all external influences here is an absolute essential. When I see others who lead less pressured existences with no full-time job to hold down in order to pay the mortgage or fewer family or other external personal involvements then I often feel envious. Bastards, do they know what it's like trying to find 30 unadulterated minutes in which to get an idea down? But then I guess I chose to be like I am.

What important influences have shaped your current interests?

Past interests inform those of the present, therefore:
Bohemianism
Jack Kerouac
The Beat Generation
The idea of poet as visionary
The inability to sing
The Blues
Bob Dylan
Big Bill Broonzy

The Futurists
Dada
Surrealism
The Bauhaus
Apollinaire
Abstract Expressionism
John Cage
Jackson Mac Low
William Wantling
Jack Spicer
John Ashbery
Clark Coolidge
Gertrude Stein
William Carlos Williams
Jean Paul Sartre
Cocteau
Standing Stones
Cymraeg
The end of the nation state
Geraint Jarman
William W. Williams, Williamstown
R.S.Thomas
Tom Petty
Philip Glass
Dion & his lonely room
Bob Cobbing
The Concrete Poets
The martial arts especially aikido, tai chi chuan and tae kwondo
Breath, Tantra, Mysticism
Tibetan Buddhism
Sharon Olds
Matsuo Basho
The BBC B
Spirals
Captain Beefheart
Duchamp
Landscape
Graffiti
Vandalism, moral panics & social disorder
Nonconformity

That place where the outgoing breath ends
and the incoming has not yet begun
Mass
The way we can turn lead into gold

What am I reading at present?
Patricia Dunker's *Hallucinating Foucault*, Paul Bowles' *Their Heads Are Green* and Charles Simic's *Frightening Toys*.

Why do some poets choose to operate from within the small press only?
There are two reasons for publishing with the small presses. Either you can't get accepted by the bigger presses, or for artistic reasons you simply don't want to bother with them. The former is easy to answer – most poets who publish over a long period end up either creeping out of the small presses (and ending up, most likely, with Bloodaxe) or they suddenly find that their small publisher has grown a bit and has acquired a new status (Arc is a fine example here). The few poets who stay small whatever do so because they like the control that small publishing offers them. Two classic cases are Ian Hamilton Finlay at his own Wild Hawthorn Press and Bob Cobbing with Writers Forum. Both poets are so idiosyncratic in their approaches that no larger press would ever be able to accommodate them. Small Presses with their antipathy towards economics, marketing and all the rest of the publishing world's regular trappings are ideal vehicles to publish a work consisting of three cards in a plastic bag or a fold out sheet with one word on it. It also helps, I guess, that the poets concerned own their respective presses.

Small is also containable within the head. Conglomerate puts form and decision in the hands of the corporate accountants. Look what happened to Chris Torrance – years of small press struggle and then, at last, grand acceptance. Paladin put him out in paperback and he was available in every bookshop UK nationwide. But that was for a mere fortnight. The company changed hands and all poetry was pulped. Famous for 15 seconds, that was Torrance's 1980 poetry fate.

Are you interested in electronic publishing?
Yes. My own web site (*http://dspace.dial.pipex.com/peter.finch*) has offered me the opportunity not only to post information about my books and what I do, but to experiment with the new form. I've set up a work called *R.S.Thomas Information* which begins as a straightforward resource for Wales' greatest living English language writer. There is some biographical detail, a bibliography, a place where you can order R.S.Thomas titles, news of his recent concerns and

then slowly you notice that the data is changing. There are hyperlinked lists of influences on R.S. His typical vocabulary is broken down and re-ordered and filled with fixed and random links. There are side leaps into descriptions of some of his recent mind-states and into critical coverage of his work (appropriately redrawn and reworked). The information (the essence of the web) becomes a new piece of creative work in itself and is then, in turn, remade to become further information as an end in itself. The form of the piece excites me considerably. It is endless and offers me infinite possibilities of change and expansion. 'The poem is never finished only abandoned' – certainly this one. And it simply cannot exist in any other medium. It's no good printing extracts in a traditional book, for example, although I guess this will end up happening.

Janet Fisher

I was pleased to be asked to do this piece, because I didn't start The Poetry Business, though I've been there ten years. I do most of the production work; but editorial decisions are made jointly between myself and Peter Sansom. He hasn't seen this, and I should say that, although we agree about most things, all views expressed here are mine and not necessarily his or the company's.

You ask is poetry in a healthy state at the moment? Is it heading nowhere? And what interests me?

There are certainly a lot of people writing poetry. Witness the quantity of poems that arrive daily at our office. Most of it can be dismissed at a glance. But there are plenty of people who know about poetry, who keep up with their reading, desperate for a publisher, but somehow not quite making it. Maybe they are trying too hard (this is more likely than not trying hard enough). Or they are engaging in some clever displacement activity instead of writing the poems they need to write, the poems that are sitting there inside them, crying out to be released.

Much of what is being published at the moment isn't very exciting. But these things go in cycles, so I'm not too worried. Ten years ago things were heaving. You couldn't step into the street without tripping over a poet (now this only happens after a night at the Albert pub poetry readings). I get a feeling that poetry is becoming institutionalised, to use a current cliché. But this is the dilemma: we (the small presses, the Poetry Society and plenty of others) have worked hard over the years to get poets recognised, to get them a living. Who would deny them this right? And yet... something's been lost in the process.

When Peter started our company in 1986 he called it The Poetry Business, to point out the ridiculous idea that anyone could make a business out of poetry. And now we do, pretty much. We pay 3 part time staff (a pittance, admittedly); we have an accountant and a business plan. Sometimes I look round the office at the computers and printers and the photocopier and the franking machine, and I feel like a small child with my miniature toy post office.

This is probably just how I am feeling at the moment. I enjoy publishing. It takes up far too much of my time which could be spent reading books and engaging in 'otium', the state of wasting time and doing nothing (and, incidentally and etymologically, the opposite of 'negotiation', the basis of business) which is the best state of mind to encourage creativity.

I don't think my writing directly informs my work as an editor. I think reading poetry informs both.

What processes lie behind my writing?

A bit like my responses here. A thought stream, a private brain-storming. Sometimes bits lie dormant in a notebook for months or years till they're ready to spring into poems. Sometimes I write from an idea, or a juxtapositioning of ideas. A recent poem called 'The day Ted died' came on because that same day John Glenn was preparing to return to space, and I was intrigued by the comparison.

After I've shuffled the words into some kind of shape I'll then put the proto-poem onto the word processor, and this gives freedom to mess about with line endings, stanza swappings, etc. It's at this point I can see if it's worth carrying on with or not. (Most aren't.) I'm not very prolific, and I do a lot of fiddly editing, mostly because I have various blind spots and tend to make grievous errors which bring me out in a cold sweat the next day when I'm revising. That's why I'd never pass a poem of mine on first writing.

What are you reading at the moment?

This immediately makes me guilty, because I am not sticking to my own nostrum (painful?) that a good writer has to read. What have I been reading lately? Not enough. Ted Hughes. Larkin. Stanley Cook (no one's heard of him; those who have rate him among the best). Many of the 'newer' poets: Armitage, Duffy, Greenlaw. Back in time to Rilke, Keats, Wordsworth. Americans: the New York poets. Bishop, Olds, Rich (especially the earlier ones), Doty, Lynch. Irish writers, too numerous to mention. The list is endless. I don't like saying who is my favourite, partly because tomorrow it will be someone else and partly because I can't face the cries of derision: '*Who*? *Him/her*?'

Sometimes I'm just so overworked and tired I can't read poetry at all. I certainly can't read it to relax at bedtime; it keeps me awake. Unless I'm ploughing through dozens of poor manuscripts, when I'm out like a light.

It is impossible, allowing time for washing and playing with my grandkids, to read all that is being published at the moment, let alone catch up with the past. *But* as an editor it's vital that I know what's going on. So I'm either selective in what I read, or I skim read (and it's an interesting phenomenon that a book always falls open at the best poems, or the ones most worth reading, as if they exerted a kind of glow that makes them unmissable; unless it's a ploy by Waterstones to make you buy the book).

Like many women I didn't start writing 'properly' till I was getting on a bit. Mid life crisis and all that (but not the usual thing). It all coincided with the mid eighties resurgence of non-Metropolitan poetry: lots of small magazines springing up, the blooming of Bloodaxe, a feeling that anything went. I can pin-point it for me with a poem in *The North* (before I joined as co-editor): Ian

McMillan's 'A Mirror Down the Toilet'. It was liberating that anyone could write about a thing like that. But it's a brilliant poem: a true imagist poem. Even thinking about it I can feel the icy wetness and the thin slivers of glass in my fingers...

Selection of work?

Most of our Smith/Doorstop writers are commissioned: people whose work we know well, who haven't got a publisher, or who need a change. They are certainly diverse; you can't get two more different writers than Michael Schmidt and Joan Jobe Smith, but we're proud to publish both. The consistency lies in their excellence in doing what they set out to do.

We run a poetry competition each year, for which, apart from a modest cash prize, the main attraction is publication, either in pamphlet or book form. We usually get 600 or 700 mss, all to be read in November and December. Of course most can be dismissed on the first page. But there is a sizeable minority which needs to be taken seriously.

As to poetry being difficult, etc:

New poets (and I know this because I used to do it myself) are often deliberately obscure and elliptical in order to sound important, and because they can't trust themselves or their poetry instincts. This is not good.

Some poets are obscure and hard to understand but it doesn't matter because the music of the words will carry the reader through; you get the meaning at a different level. All good poems should do this, so in a sense it doesn't matter whether they are superficially 'easy' or not, if they have the underlying resonance which makes it worth reading again and again. A poet has to write in her/his own idiom and poems can take many paths.

I don't think 'difficult' poets will ever be 'popular' in the sense of winning Poems Of The Year contests and such like. As I write we are waiting, breaths baited, to see who will be anointed Poet Laureate. One early contender who was soon dismissed was Geoffrey Hill. The general public have possibly never heard of him. His work is elliptical, full of allusive references, rigorous, demanding, ultimately satisfying. But popular, no.

Some good modern poets are popular. I would contend that this popularity, so far as the general public are concerned, depends as much on their personality, or power of presentation, or on the other things they write, as on the quality of their poetry, which most people won't have read. This doesn't detract from their poetry, which is still good, and indeed the other aspects would be pointless and the poets themselves wouldn't be worth taking seriously, if the poems they wrote weren't good. And in fact this popularity can have an adverse effect on their reputation among so-called serious critics, who might think that because a poet is 'popular' they can't really be 'good'.

So to be 'good' isn't necessarily the same as 'popular'. And vice versa. I could draw you a Venn diagram to illustrate this, but apparently these are no longer on the Maths syllabus. A pity, as they were one of the few mathematical concepts I could understand.

The motivating forces behind poetry publishing?

The job itself. I worked as an editorial assistant in London in the early 70s. Gave it up to have kids. When I moved north I gave up all hope of ever getting back into publishing. Now I run my own company. Modern technology means we can compete with large publishers in terms of production; we have reps and distributors; I am learning all the time how to produce better books and how to publicise them. I am very lucky; I have the freedom to write my own job description. The Poetry Business receives reasonable grant aid, but we've worked for it over the past 13 years, slaving away at the book face. And our competition brings in an extra wadge, which goes back into printing costs, or equipment, or maybe even wages. That's the rub: it's not possible to earn a living wage, and I couldn't do it if I wasn't a kept woman, but that's another story...

One advantage of being small and subsidised is that we don't have to worry about shareholders and financial directors (our grant aid applications always seem to me the equivalent of a company report to shareholders and need to be just as upbeat and convincing). In fact we are positively encouraged to publish writers who wouldn't find a voice anywhere else, not because they aren't good, but because we can take the risk on them which a mainstream publisher can't afford to, or isn't inclined to do. This is not to say that we wouldn't welcome a best-seller if it appeared on our doorstop.

Because we have a small list we can afford to offer our writers a hands-on editorial approach, plus lashings of TLC; partly because we want their work to be the best it can be, and partly because we like our writers and want to be kind to them.

But our main motivating force is a love of good poetry, followed by the excitement that's generated when we come across a real writer; and the pleasure when this is acknowledged by critics and reviewers, even though there may not be very large sales.

Society, politics, gender?

The subject of a poem can be about anything (see Ian's Toilet poem, above). The poem is usually about the poet's relationship with the rest-of-the-world (including herself). Contexts don't really matter. If there is genuine concern, involvement, anger. love, etc., social issues are as valid a subject as anything else. The trouble is, there is often a knee jerk response to emotive issues displayed prominently on TV (war, child abuse etc); 'writing as therapy' has its place, but not in our post bag please. There are clichés in subject matter just as much as in language. Leave writing about news events to journalists; they do it so much better.

As to sexual politics: impossible to ignore. Women are often condemned for writing 'domestic' poems. If men do it it's regarded as brave and challenging. There's as much muck and sweat in the conventional kitchen as there is on the shop floor or the football field, or the pub, or whatever places are regarded as male preserves. I was praised once for writing about driving badly on a motorway. That's all very well. Look around you, fellers, and see who's running the show, then get your pens out.

As to women's anthologies, I've been in several, so I'm not going to argue this point. Perhaps I should have some pride and not be in them. But I'm not well known enough for it to matter. No one's going to pick up the next women's anthology and say 'gosh, why isn't Janet Fisher in it? She must be making a stand, good for her.' If they thought anything at all it would be that I just wasn't important enough to have been asked. I know some women refuse to be in them. I like and admire that. I'm just selfishly joining the scrabble for a minimal share of attention. But in no way do I want to be regarded as a 'woman-poet'.

One of the most well known poetry editors in recent times was a woman, and she's just been kicked in the teeth by a male establishment.

As a Female-Eunuch-style feminist I would say the personal **is** the political: the seamless web theory. And I don't mean my tights.

Anthologies?

I don't usually read them, they're often predictable and boring. One of the recent best is The Emergency Kit, which concentrates on the poem rather than the poet and contains gems we might otherwise have missed. The main advantage of general anthologies is as an introduction for new readers who don't know where to start, a bit like the set menus in Thai restaurants.

Visual... aural... oral?

Poetry exists all around us. Listen to people in the street, on the bus. The natural rhythm of English speech is the iambic pentameter and its variations. 'I haven't seen a single soul all day'. 'They say it's gonna rain again tomorrow'. 'We are the masters now, so pay attention.' etc., etc.

The bizarre, the surreal, too, are there for the picking. It takes the genius of someone like Ian McMillan to pick and transform these gleanings into something we've never thought about but knew was there all along.

But it needs to be worn lightly. 'He who catch the joy as it flies...' etc. It doesn't all have to be written down in a book, or performed on a stage.

I think however that poetry in the current Western convention, when it comes to be written (and why not, if it isn't we're all out of a job) must succeed primarily on the page. It's good if it can be read aloud as well. If a poem has metre, assonance, rhyme, it *should* be read aloud. Also, it's good to hear the poet's own voice reading it. It's often a way of getting a handle on a poet whose work has previously eluded you.

But ultimately all poetry harks back to the rhythms of speech, the beat of the heart, the pulse in the womb, however we may attenuate, expand, divert. We need those echoes. Otherwise it's cut-up prose, stand-up comedy.

Changes in the way poets operate?

Don't like this word 'operate'. Are we to write our poems to fit in with the medium? Why not? Poets have always done this. Commissions are not a bad thing. They can often make you write things you wouldn't otherwise have written. Poems don't always have to be *inspired* by personal emotions. A friend of mine has just been commissioned to write a poem to appear in chip shops in a certain area. The resulting poem is not only as good a chip shop poem as I've ever read, but is intensely personal and evocative and extremely well written.

If good poems can appear in chip shops, or on tube trains and buses, or handed out in the street or splashed up on buildings, is this not all to the good? It (a) brings in more readers; and (b) possibly sells more books.

Why still publish books in the electronic age?

I think this is an old chestnut. Whatever happened to the paperless office? I spend hours a day in front of my computer, till my head's buzzing. The last thing I want to do is read poetry off a screen; I might forget and start to run the spell check. You can't curl up in bed or the bath with a screen. Also books don't just look good, they feel good and smell good, and they don't make that horrid humming noise; don't know what they taste like.

Computers play an important part in publishing. My golden rule is never type anything in more than once. I can put a pamphlet together in half a day, provided the poet was thoughtful enough to have transcribed their poetry onto a word processor; and even scanning in a manuscript takes only a few hours longer. Working with printers now is so much more convenient; it was only a few years ago we were pasting up with cowgum, and if you're astigmatic it's hard to get things straight.

We hope soon to be part of an on-line bookshop for the small presses, but this will have to offer a better informed service than the major ones, or why shouldn't people just go to amazon dot com for listings? We don't use any poetry sites. I've sussed out one or two, but though it might be interesting to chat with other writers about poetry and why the Poetry Society's website is down *again*, it seems to me like another sort of displacement activity, and if so I'd rather read a thriller or watch *Eastenders*.

Linda France

A Fortnight in the Life of...

The truth is what I think sometimes, on some days, about some things
— Marguerite Duras

Monday 8th February 1999

Maybe the best way to begin is like this, on the long train journey from Newcastle to Exeter. I know I'm resisting answering the questions Andy suggested for this book, unwilling to commit myself to opinions I know are largely irrelevant and will certainly change in response to shifts in situations and moods. But I like writing on trains: the sense of being in a capsule in nowhere time, the rhythm, the absence of domestic distractions. And today it seems to suit my reluctance to pin myself down.

I spend part of the journey finishing off a version of a Lorca poem I've been working on, *Gacela del Amore Imprevisto*, worrying about the liberties I've taken and wishing I had the courage to take more. I look up and see a very large sign painted on a gate – *Dogs Loose Day and Night*. I can practically hear them howl.

There's an article in the paper about why our brains need art – the pleasure principle. I love hearing my own opinions confirmed by scientists. For a long time now in writing workshops I've been encouraging students to approach their subjects from the angle of pleasure to work up some energy, some passion. If *they're* interested in their theme, there's more chance the reader will be too. This sounds obvious, but for some reason when it comes to writing a poem, many people seem to think they have to be either very serious or very flippant and they forget about the power of pleasure.

Eventually I manage to write four pages of my thoughts on contemporary poetry but I feel impatient with my own style, which drags like a train that's very slow, very late. Ruthless, all I want to retain is a quote from Selima Hill: 'I call poetry, not the latest Faber book, just a sense of the present moment... the best thing about writing poetry is the same as the best thing about being alive.'

Saturday 13th February

The train journey home from Totleigh Barton, where I've been teaching a School's Course, feels shorter and less tortured than the journey down. I feel satisfied and changed by my week's work. We talked a lot about the old Poetry vs. Prose argument and even though I want to say it's all the same, it's all language, I still feel alienated by all those words, the tyranny of narrative. Although my co-tutor, novelist James Friel, introduces me to a seductive little form, its inventor, Dan Rhodes, calls 'dwarves' – very short (100 words) prose pieces on the theme of relationships. Pithy. Amusing. I write one on the train called *The Cornishman*. 100 words I can just about cope with. In fact I enjoy the utter lack of ornamentation, the focus it seems to elicit. They remind me of Peter Reading's 100 x 100 worders in his collection *C*.

Our visiting writer, Stephen Knight, has just written a novel. He speaks about his disenchantment with poetry as a genre. How small the world is, the fact that poetry is only read by other poets. That night Mammon sat on my pillow and whispered in my ear till dawn. Stephen said that he turned to fiction because he found there were certain themes he wasn't addressing, certain ideas that just didn't formulate themselves into poems. Thinking about that I'm aware that my work doesn't reveal as much social concern as I actually experience. This perpetuates the view that poetry has become too introspective, limited in its vision, disconnected from 'the real world'. I felt this particularly keenly this week, working with 16 – 18 year olds, hearing *their* experiences of *their* worlds, their responses to it – the pressures of school, broken homes, smoking and drinking and sexuality, varying degrees of self-mutilation.

On the train I read Saturday's *Valentine Guardian* stuffed full of recommended love poems. As well as a big splash on John Berger. Also a piece by Don Paterson on self-education. This raises my spirits and banishes the prose sirens for the time being. Poetry is dead! Long Live Poetry! I'm going home to my sweetheart and, heigh nonny no, all is very well indeed.

Thursday 18th February

Last night I was booked to do a session on 'Working as a Poet' for the M.A. in Creative Writing at the University of Northumbria; basically about how I earn a living. When I was asked to do this my bank account was less than healthy and I laughed at the irony of it. The idea is to *encourage* the students, to let them know that it is possible. The module's called 'The Writing Industry', which is less of a joke than it sounds. Fortunately – for them and for me – now the situation has improved and I'm feeling positive and busy and although not financially secure, solvent and expectant. I am used to the cyclical, erratic nature of a poet's income but that still doesn't stop me indulging in serious fantasies about 'a proper job' when I'm at a low ebb.

One student repeatedly asked me irrelevant questions, interesting but out of place. The other students started to look uncomfortable and I ended up having to tell her point blank that I was there to speak about my writing as a profession and it wasn't appropriate for me to read new work or talk about my poetic process. She didn't like this and made a big show of packing up her things and a quarter of an hour before the end announced that I seemed to be saying that poetry is a game and I know how to play it: I've won and others have lost. This, after I've talked in an open and trusting way about the demands, the responsibilities and the sacrifices of a poet's life. Essentially she was asking me to justify my existence. I chose to do so as graciously as possible, feeling rattled but managing to look composed.

This sort of thing is no doubt one of the reasons why Larkin kept his job as a librarian and was reluctant to go around the country pretending to be himself. It certainly left me thinking what has this to do with poetry? Is it worth it? Generally I get a lot of satisfaction from working with groups although I have had my fair share of nightmares. It was fortuitous that today I met with my older people's group in Hexham and their freshness and enthusiasm, untainted by an excess of ego and ambition, worked as a healthy corrective to last night's craziness.

As I get older I become more and more impatient with cleverness, self-consciousness, contrivance, lack of straightforwardness. I want poetry that is willing to go beyond itself, to edge in the direction of change, to take risks, positive risks, not negative ones. I don't want poetry that forgets it's essentially song, that it's job is to get one over on Auden and make something happen, change something, even if it's only something small in the mind and heart of a single individual. One of the most satisfying compliments I ever had after a reading was that my poems (in this instance, the prostitution poems in *Storyville*) weren't trying to be entertaining. I liked that. Poetry is not a joke. It's not a leisure activity. Unlike football, it isn't more important than life or death, but it's still one of the few places we have left where we can hear the birth cry and the death rattle and know it's our own.

There I've done it. I've pinned myself down. I've committed myself. So I realise the reason why I was reluctant was because poetry matters so much to me, I can hardly articulate what I feel about it. Which is also one of the reasons I am a poet – that compulsion to define your position against the fragile, dynamic counterpoint of an awareness of the inadequacy, the terrible power of the word.

Friday 19th February

Today I have a meeting with Claire Malcolm, director of New Writing North, Northern Arts' Literature Agency, and Vikki Bennett, a young poet from Cumbria. Claire has asked me if I will act as a mentor for Vikki, guide her and encourage her. Vikki and I have met before, briefly, at a reading I gave in Penrith a couple of years ago. I warmed to her immediately so working with her over a six-month period doesn't seem a burdensome prospect. It's just the sort of challenge I enjoy – a degree of responsibility and risk, the possibility of profound communication and transformation. On both sides.

It strikes me not for the first time how much easier it is to locate other people's strengths and weaknesses than it is your own. I wish I'd had a mentor when I first started writing for an audience. In fact sometimes I wish I had one now – the poetry equivalent of a personal trainer to keep me motivated and on top form. Luckily I have my own whip-cracking sub-personality who keeps the show on the road, but how good it would be to surrender, to share some of the intensity. This reminds me that I'm meeting up with Jo Shapcott, currently Northern Arts Literary Fellow, next week. I think I'll suggest to her we might do some poem-swapping for feedback and stimulation purposes. Once you're published and established you're expected to do more nourishing than being nourished. Who mothers the mother?

I *have* been nourished reading Joan Johnston's *What You Want,* a Diamond Twig publication (edited by Julia Darling and Ellen Phethean in Newcastle) launched at Dillons a couple of weeks ago. It's just a little book and the poems are little poems, but they pack a powerful punch. Joan's voice is very individualistic, quirky, playful, fascinated with time and memory, what lasts and what doesn't. And with frocks. The new collection I'm currently working on is going under the name of *The Simultaneous Dress,* so I'm right there in the Ladies' Fashions Department of the Poetry Store that Joan evokes with such precision and delight, aware of the significance of clothes, the way they can be an extension of personality and experience.

By one of those happy coincidences that maybe aren't at all, but just a neurotic need to make connections between one's disparate experiences, this same week a friend has given me a book of photographs by J.H. Lartigue, a selection reflecting his love of women. And what women – so chic and gorgeous, all frocked and hatted and brooched and stockinged and shod with a remarkable combination of attention to detail and easy grace. The way I'd like my poems to be. I'm hoping that the photographs and Joan's poems will inspire me to write more 'simultaneous dress' poems for the collection. The last time I looked at it there were more house poems than dress poems. Both houses and garments are for me symbols of the extended body but the house has become too distant for my current purposes. I want more skin contact. The impulse of the book is to bring the different ways we live closer together to achieve an integrity of intention and action, reflected in the idea of the artist Sonia Delaunay's 'simultaneous dress', designed to reflect the wearer's shape and movement.

The process of reviewing the work in progress is absorbing but fragile, gradually discovering what it is I seem to be doing in my poems at the moment and if that's different from what I want to do. It's paradigmatic of what happens sometimes with an individual poem when you're trying to find out what you think or feel about something: only in the act of writing does it become clear. Only in the process of compiling a collection do you really see what colour it is, what the prevailing cut is. This book is nearing completion so I can see it more clearly than previously. It's taking on a shape of its own and I'm making a feature of it by my own fussy tweakings, my mouth full of pins.

Looking back, I wish I'd had a bit more time for tweaking when I was editing *Sixty Women Poets*. I'm returning to the M.A. course in a month's time to speak about how I put the anthology together. It's being used as a set text but has been out of print for over a year; frustrating for everyone, although Bloodaxe tell me it's being reprinted, for the third time, in May. I'm delighted it is still popular, still considered relevant. It was always intended as a survey of women's poetry in Britain and Ireland since 1971, an important record of women's work across the subsequent two decades. For this reason I regret not representing two poets who I consider important but whose work at the time I felt ambivalent about – Kathleen Raine and Ruth Fainlight. Given more time to reflect, I think they would have been included at the expense of a few of the more minor poets represented. I stand by my choice of the poems themselves; they all work well and deserve inclusion but in terms of a wider view of the poet's importance, I think there could be a few changes.

The aspect of the book I found most challenging at the time was the selection of the newer poets who'd maybe only published a single collection; this was always pushing the limits of the brief, but I wanted it to feel current as well as taking a look back. It was difficult in some cases to predict what would endure and again I went simply on what I responded to positively at the time. I think this is the editor's prerogative and is usually what gives an anthology (or magazine) individuality and bite. However I regret not including poems by Sarah Maguire and Susan Wicks, two poets who I've come to admire but then failed to appreciate their oddly direct subtlety.

I'm aware my tastes have changed and I'm less concerned that poems should be straight-forward, single-minded and accessible. For *Sixty Women Poets* I often chose poems that went out of their way to be provocative in terms of *what* they were saying but now I want to read poems that are original, striking and rebellious in *the way* they're written, retaining evidence of single-mindedness, but in a more eccentric, less predictable way. I've also come to appreciate the rebellion of *not* being striking, *not* aiming to please – a truly revolutionary act for women, poets or otherwise.

While there are so many poets writing now, so much being published, I particularly enjoy coming across someone who stands out in some way, who is doing something different, whose work changes the way I think about things. The collection by a woman I most enjoyed last year was the Canadian Anne Carson's *Glass and God.* I was fascinated by her rhythms, the blatant waywardness of her thought processes, her strange juxtapositions, confident handling of free form and clarity of tone and expression. For not dissimilar reasons I currently admire the work of Ida Affleck Graves, Alice Oswald, Katherine Pierpoint and Katrina Porteous. Sometimes it's hard to tell if something is a cause or an effect but I'd like to think that while it celebrated a renaissance in women's poetry, *Sixty Women Poets* also brought fresh energy to fuel the flowering. Since 1993 there's been a positive torrent of new work by women, often by *new* women. Maura Dooley's *Making For Planet Alice* showcased some of these.Time will tell how the work in this book wears, which poets are still publishing, still making an impact. It does seem that female poets are more visible, more confident and possibly more appreciated than they were six years ago but they are still not accorded equal status with male poets. There's still some way to go.

Saturday 20th February

Today I pick up a copy of *The Northern Review*, our local arts listing magazine. The 'Sound-Off' feature this month is by Mark Robinson on the *Book of the North*, a CD Rom collaboration he took part in last year with me and thirteen other poets, novelists and visual artists. As he says, '15 is a good number for rugby union but not for artistic collaboration.' It's funny reading his version of events which is enthusiastic, flag-waving even, although shamelessly bemused at times: 'It should be fun to use, will project brilliantly on the walls of literature venues, and contains some fascinating work by many of the North's leading writers and artists.' Put like that who needs to worry about understanding the damn thing.

We were all more or less bemused at different times working on this project. The meetings left me feeling dizzy. So many ideas, so few connections. I also wasn't keen to become more involved in the technological side of things, considering it tangential to my current concerns. This was one of the positive benefits of the large numbers engaged in the project: it meant this was okay and a few of us stuck with the traditional formula of words on the page, while others took on the medium as a real influence on the work they produced. What affected my contribution was the experience of working with so many diverse creative personalities in what sometimes felt like an unnatural, exposed way. Thinking and working with little sense of centre, of certainty, meant I produced quite dark work for much of the process. Hardly surprising when the setting that evolved was *Underland*, a strange society with some unfathomable geographical connection with True North. Some of us even spent a day down an old lead mine, an amazing experience, terrifying and magical. If nothing good comes of *Book of the North*, I'm grateful to it for that.

When it came down to putting the whole thing together in some kind of coherent way, it was considered that the general mood was *too* dark. The editorial committee deemed me a good person to lighten it up a bit and asked me to write a series of 'upbeat' poems about *Hotel Throat*. I'd already been working with prose writers Bridget O'Connor, Julia Darling and Margaret Wilkinson on this particular strand so I knew just how weird it was turning out to be.

I wrote the poems in a business-like fashion, working to a deadline, but appreciated permission to be affirming. Or as affirming as I could be in a hotel the Coen brothers would be proud of. They came out clotted and slightly crazy, intoxicated with language and ideas. They're tight-rope walking poems, bristling with tension, odd perspectives and immense exhilaration. I know I would never have written any of these poems without the stimulation of the collaboration. Even the difficult bits. They were probably vital. And some of them have ended up in my new book, which is a bonus. I like the sense that they have more than one life, that they can appear in different guises.

This isn't always the case for some of the collaborations I've been involved in. I'm thinking particularly of the Public Art commissions I've worked on. Because these are site-specific and written taking into account the medium and structure of the piece – wood, stone, stained glass or whatever – they rarely translate easily to the page. Also because I write these after consultation with the local community and try to reflect their interests and aspirations, these poems don't work as 'book poems'. They're too occasional, too three-dimensional, too *al fresco*. I like that too: poems spilling beyond the covers of a book to reach a wider audience, uncollected.

Monday 22nd February

This morning after two hours all I've come up with are two limping lines of a villanelle I'm trying to write about my youngest son, which I hope will translate as *every* mother's son. He's going through his 'difficult' teenage years, but I seem to be finding it more difficult than he is. We had a particularly dramatic interaction on Saturday night so, as usual in response to powerful experiences, I am moved to write about it. I chose the villanelle form to act as a check on the strong emotions, hoping it will both contain and channel what I'm trying to convey: the way you can't contain and channel another human being even if, especially if, you gave birth to him. I have a vivid vision of what I want this poem to do but only a vague one of *how*. At the moment I think perhaps I'm too close and a bit blocked but I so want to try to catch it while it's fresh and at the front of my mind.

I also have an ulterior, less maternal, motive. I'm writing a series of features on poetic form for *Mslexia*, the new magazine for women writers, and my next choice of form is the villanelle. In the first issue I concentrated on the sonnet and was able to use a couple from an unpublished sequence of Selima Hill's. The idea is that in every edition I explain the technicalities and potential of a different fixed form and use a new poem to illustrate specific points. It's an excellent means of commissioning new work by women as well as demystifying the practicalities of craft.

Even though I've written several villanelles before, it's a form I have problems with, finding it elusive in itself: difficult to sustain and convey a natural tone within the constraints of the repetitions and rhyme. But I also know what it's capable of; one of my favourite poems is Elizabeth Bishop's *One Art*, a consummate example. Maybe that's why I'm always dissatisfied with my attempts at villanelles – they never match hers. But having strong positive models is vital and I enjoy the challenge and will definitely keep on trying. Just not today. Tomorrow everything will look different and I'll be able to write a different poem.

John Kinsella

'Stolen from Stein'

We meet in a coffee shop on Trinity Street. I offer to buy but he declines. He already has an orange juice and doesn't eat during the day. They don't serve vegan food here, he adds. I ask him what's going on in contemporary poetry that interests you? He stares at the table. I like the fax machine, he answers. I like the way it encrypts and decodes. You work a lot through the internet these days. Good for collaboration but it generates nothing in itself – it's illusory, though in some ways I guess I'm addicted. He doesn't want to say more than this. You've written a lot about hybridity. From a post-colonial theory point of view and a textual one. Yes, but I get annoyed with confusion between cross-over and 'hybridity' – the latter has a specific set of politics attached to it. As much as the word itself generates the poem, so does 'hybridity' generate political discourse. Go read Homi Bhabha for starters. For a moment I think he's being arrogant, but then realise he's taking the piss out of himself as much as anything else. He says: I've not been too well lately, though I put a good face on it. Am I looking for congratulations, admiration? I feel like I'm in a Browning narrative sometimes, or caught in a pallid pre-Raphaelite painting. Now there you'll find the woman-as-object, the fetishisation thing at its most extreme, most appalling. Gender is a problem for me. As a male I'm privileged enough to say something so trite. My father was out of the picture early on. I take on the persona of a woman – Lilith for one, I've another brewing. One of the Macbeth witches. Isn't language fun! The irony almost stings the sense... It is impossible to write a poem without an awareness of the implication of gender: persona, the patriarchal nature of the canon, the question of relevance. Who is the audience for a poem? Look, this poem is written in perfect terza rima and should be used as a model for good verse. Says who. Yes, Language poetry gave me the boost I needed a decade ago – finally, something taking the lyrical voice to task in a 'systematic' way. Maybe it was a hangover from my Marxist teens. I ditched that for Kropotkin. I'm still an anarchist. I noted that he was clean-shaven and that his clothes were freshly laundered. He was dressed in black. American denim. He corrects me – Australian denim, my mother sends them. Language is moving into its post- period. Reinventing the lyric. A poet like Susan Howe was doing that from the beginning. She's always been a lyrical innovator. One shouldn't divorce the lyric from the political implications of language-usage. In fact, it's impossible to. The lyric doesn't have to be ego-tagged, to be caught in the 'romantic' lyrical-I framework. Interestingly, many lyrics condemned as being of the authoritative self were revolutionary breakthroughs in their time – liberating and invigorating language. Look at Lyrical Ballads for starters. Anyway, for me it all comes from Gertrude Stein's *Rose is a rose is a rose is a rose*. I write, or is this your piece of paper? You wrote it? Really, thanks for bringing it along. So, you also like Stein. And know Australia – the south-west of Australia – my part of the world. Though I live here now. I'd swear this was set in York – seventy miles outside of Perth. About 110 ks. Yes, the place names really get you don't they. The signifier for death. For the process of occupation and (re) territorialisation. Can I read it aloud? Do you mind? I'm sure the other people in the shop would find it of interest. Ironic, isn't it. A poem by a Brit on an Australian place using Gertrude Stein as a reference point. Being read aloud by an Australian from that place who lives here now, whose daughter now has a Cambridge accent. Town or gown? A mixture of both, I think. Okay, I'll read it:

Rose is a rose is a rose is a rose

From Rose Hill the town
is both large and small –
it is a thing of the eye
and there's nothing complex
about it: a flock of white cockatoos
implodes to a point of singularity,
before pluming out over the football field,
town hall, a stand of trees
without a name. It's the paradox
of place: always the variety,
the pleasant conflict of styles.
The rose, the cockatoo,
the failure of colour as whiteness
merges with sunlight.

What important influences have shaped your current interests?

Working on the *Poems* of J.H. Prynne for the last three years. Not only my work but my life. And trying to develop an objective correlative system that works both in the fens landscape and the wheatbelt landscape of Western Australia. Exile and home. I don't know what home is. Who am I to 'own'? My family own land. They've got the title deeds. I've been reading title deeds and house plans lately. I'm drawing sketches for poems. And editing *Tristram Shandy* – that infinite number of books packaged as one. That's what the net pretends to offer poetry – hyperspatiality. The metaphor beat it to it. Though it's interesting creating a kind of negative feedback through hypertext and metaphor. We all rewrite the same poems. I draft a lot. They're all finished poems. A painting is a poem, music is a poem – a collaboration with a sound artist has recently hit the shelves. A cd and photos and text. About a virus – maybe human-made – wiping out kangaroos. It's starting to rain outside. Visited Heffers? he asks. Should while you're here. Great poetry section. Recently bought Zukofsky's *Collected Shorter Poems*. The net breaks the buying cycle, and that's good. His orange juice lasts longer than it should. You see yourself as belonging to no camp? No, but it strikes me that camps are more often created by critics than poets. Or maybe poets when they're not together. Get them in one room and they're usually polite to each other's faces. Hypocrisy? Is that what you're suggesting? Not really – just that quite often debates have more to do with territory than language.

Earlier you introduced your father, Lilith and questions of gender. Can you expand?

I've always wondered about the expression 'brought up in a household of women'. The absence of the patriarch, the eldest boy become head of the house and being over-invested with 'fatherly values', or conversely, being manufactured as either a 'mother's boy' – unable to take his place within the patriarchy, or a mother's revenge on the male world which left her in this state of aloneness. Of course, 'a household of women' might mean a conspiracy of sisters, or a bench of aunts, a commune of women, or a woman-to-woman relationship. Whichever of these is specific to the conditions under which I wrote and indeed still write, in some way a consciousness of all these has influenced and continues to influence my work. I have a father, but he is absent or cross-dressed.

Lilith – first Eve in Hebrew myth – was appropriated as vengeful mother by me at an early date. The symbolism of Eve herself seemed to wrapped up in male wish-fulfilment, too much a propaganda exercise. The seed penetrating the egg, the passive deployment of the female body, the berkertex bride (or 'bribe', *à la* Crass) implications of the exile from the Garden seemed conveniently aimed toward male empowerment. That Eve in fact fell to temptation rather than being implicitly evil seemed part of this. Lilith, on the other hand, was an emasculator – created from mud and dirt, she was the vengeful mother who copulated with demon spawn, who took her vengeance on males in their unfaithful dreams, who played the hand of guilt, who took God on despite everything, who challenged the sanctity of the first-born. I hated and loved her for this. As male, as first-born. And for me, she was the symbol of the power of language.

The Lilith Poems began as a collaboration with an Australian artist and sculptor, Mona Ryder. We were invited to work together on something called The Bookworks exhibition at the Perth Institute of Contemporary Art. I told Mona of the Lilith myth and she sparked – producing dozens of etchings and drawings which worked as parallel 'texts' to a sequence of poems I was developing. Interestingly enough, we abandoned Lilith with regard to Bookworks because the project grew too large, settling instead on a work entitled *The Book of Two Faces*, which explores similar issues, the text of which is now included in *Poems 1980-1994*. Lilith itself went on to become a book but my publishers opted to integrate my texts into *Eschatologies* because of the expense of producing a book with artwork. Mona ended up displaying her artwork at the Queensland State Library with some hand-written poems to accompany it. The questions of gender identity that the poems explore are obvious, and are best stated by the poems themselves. Primary among them is the irony implicit in the presentation of a female voice by a male poet-persona as unstable and self-reflexive. In the end we have a 'queer' rather than a female voice, and the male poet is deconstructed into the mouthpiece of patriarchy that it is, regardless of good intentions. Humour, the red herring-for the male poet to laugh at himself, doesn't suppress – if that's the right word – his complicity in patriarchal oppressiveness.

Two poems from *Full Fathom Five* develop the Lilith theme further, but more in terms of aesthetics and popular culture. 'Sexual Politics in Eadweard Muybridge's *Man Walking After Traumatism of the Head*' and 'On Andy Warhol's *Marilyn Six-Pack*' are investigations of art and movement – cultural and physical. In both poems the father is cross-dressed and transformed into cultural icon, playing against received notions of male identity. Eadweard Muybridge is seen as a 'father' of cinema, Andy Warhol as a 'father' of pop art, The Velvet Underground, and the motivation for Valerie Solanas. It is interesting to consider the Factory members' Freudian take on the Solanas shooting of Warhol – as parricide. At the basis of both poems is the issue of fetishisation, of making consumables out of the body and art. The connection between 'woman' and 'art' – the product, not the process – being, of course, in patriarchy, undeniable. Through these poems, ironical as they might be, it is still male art we're receiving. The Warhol poem is an unrhymed, semi-metred sonnet. It breaks down the binary between structure as a name and structure as a pragmatic device, but still it is a victim of history, of art, of the aesthetic. As is Marilyn, of course. She is the poem, is Warhol, is the audience. The author is dead, but so is the subject matter. And the value of the corpse is rising daily, at least at the moment.

Elements of the issues explored in my poetry carry across to my fiction, though in some ways the project is more obvious in the latter. In my novel *Genre* I interweave different narrative threads and visual motifs into a single paragraph that runs for over 300 pages. The devices at work are appropriation, monologue, dialogue, discourse, the letter, translation, word-games, rhizomic linguistic tropes, and so on. The prime concerns are gender and representation – the body of text, the corporeality of place, the machine of the page and so on. The novel is set in a block of flats which work like a Venn diagram, the lives of the occupants interacting, resisting, colliding, functioning with apparent indifference – though, in a sense, 'adding up'. The unifying theme is surveillance and censorship. What can we or do we hear or see of their lives? Is what we're presented – in whichever voice or narrative mode is networking at the time – in fact 'truth'? Abjection, censorship, and pornography are recurring themes. Or maybe the only themes.

Which brings me to Eros. Not a god, and not about love. Rather, a propaganda tool. A pastoral construct. Like those figureheads of the patriarchy: Britannia, Mother Earth, Marianne, Liberty. The book subverts such constructions. Male and female become biological terms, templates for experience and that variable 'truth'. The book has already created controversy in Australia where it was published last November. A friend recently e-mailed me to ask what my 'intention' was behind one of the stories (one of the 'milder' ones) – 'The Throats of Foxes'. This is my reply:

The story is actually based on a personal ad I read in a magazine called *Sex News* (research, honestly!) in which the advertiser was offering potions made from the urine of pregnant women to increase sex drive etc (pre-Viagra...). It was also asking for pregnant women to write to a P.O. box if they were interested in becoming 'donors'. The ad also offered other witchcraft-related paraphernalia and often talked of 'animal prowess' etc. Thus the fox connection. And it is true that the fox does scream like a human – I've heard it many times. The connection between the pagan fertility ritual, death, and the 'animal' comes together at the end. There's a kind of lycanthropic process taking place, a transformation not into something else, but an awakening of the latent.

Rupert Loydell

What's going on in contemporary poetry that interests you?

Most of the poetry I currently enjoy seems to be marginalised and a long way from the colloquial or jokey schools of narrative which have become the accepted norm within 'mainstream' poetry publishing. I am drawn more towards the work of American poets like Mark Strand, Charles Wright, Jorie Graham, Stephen Berg and Charles Simic – who are certainly 'mainstream' over there, as well as towards some of the more linguistically innovative work happening in Britain. I still enjoy reading writers such as Ken Smith and Robert Creeley, who you might argue are not 'contemporary'. More and more I find myself going sideways or backwards to poets, often dead, such as John Berryman, W.S. Graham and David Jones – as often as not writing about the spiritual as well as pushing form around. I also find myself in a minority who read the work of Robert Lax, William Everson, Gavin Bantock – again, authors with a spiritual as much as linguistic agenda.

I am open to all sorts of poetry, but want the work to be working with language anew. I am sick to death of the poem that is a kind of shaggy-dog story, where once you get the joke or punch-line that's it. This seems to be most of what the 'gritty Northern Realist' school consisted of – of course, as a style it's now spread to all points of the compass, so I don't mean to be regionalist here. I'm also less and less moved by passionate, even exquisitely worked, lyrical poems that somehow try to 'share' something with us. But I also find the really experimental end of poetry as dull as ditchwater. Where the language has become sterilised and cut-up or dropped onto the page as 'object', with no regard for the music of the work. Writers such as Ken Edwards, Alan Halsey, Gavin Selerie, Drew Milne, Sheila Murphy, Clark Coolidge and many others seem to avoid falling into that coldness of language. I particularly enjoyed reading the Talisman House *An Anthology of New (American) Poets* recently, and dipping into *Conductors of Chaos* when that came out – though in the end I probably dislike more of the poetry than I like in the latter. I enjoy performance poetry if it makes me laugh and entertains me when I'm watching, but it's not for me on the page.

Is poetry in a healthy state at the moment, or is it heading nowhere?

Poetry is as healthy as it can be. Publishing activity and sales of poetry are very unhealthy. The 'New Generation' marketing exercise seems to have created a new canon of extremely dull writers, widely accepted and praised by editors and critics; these writers and their imitators seem to be clogging up the editorial offices and published output of most of the mainstream poetry houses. We are also suffering from creative writing syndrome, with everyone being told they have something to say and the means to say it. I'm all for creative writing, all for reading, even for a bit of therapy sometimes – but it has to go hand-in-hand with a critical development; this simply isn't happening. Poetry has become something every Tom, Dick or Harry now thinks they can do – without reading any poetry or learning to edit themselves.

But, of course, just because so-and-so's poetry list is dull doesn't mean that all around the world great poetry isn't happening. Language is being played with, changed, shaped, used and abused as I write this; poetry is changing, mutating and evolving – and very healthy it is, too, though many of us may not understand or enjoy much of it as it happens.

What chances and risks are taken in your own work, or the work you have edited/published?

With regard to my own writing, I am always aware that someone else has probably gone further, pushed harder, or arrived at the same place by another route; so the 'chances and risks' are simply *personal* ones. They would involve new processes, new ways to edit, taking on board what I've been reading or discussing recently: perhaps cut-ups, numerical or alphabetical systems, combining several poems in to one. I'm also aware that much of my writing is a kind of 'open' writing which – however much fiction and creating is involved – still seems to have elements of personal confession and biography in it. I try to be 'honest' and clear in my work, which is sometimes difficult within experimental form. Clarity remains a guiding principle, with a commitment to everyday vocabulary. I want people to understand the actual words and shape of the sentence they form, even if by new contextualising or unusual usage, the meaning or shape of the poem may prove more elusive.

I am aware, too, that putting out many types of writing is a sort of risk – both for myself, and as Stride. But that openness can work for us as well as against us. I believe Stride has made some types of writing – the prose-poem for instance, various 'experimental' American writers – more accessible by contextualising them, and also by showing the lineage of various types of poetry (as well as sideways relationships between 'schools') and by publishing alternative and varied ways of 'saying the same thing'. I would hope people who read Stride titles find things they would not if they deal with a publisher with a very particular slant. Whilst Stride has probably never been consistently 'cutting edge' or 'avant garde' I *do* believe we showcase a wide variety of writing that takes many chances and risks. These of course can be as much publishing an unknown author working in free verse or Colin Falck's use of the sonnet as some crazy linguistic cut-up new writing!

What processes lie behind the writing of your poems? How much editing and rewriting goes into your own poetry?

I still need to be inspired to write, whether or not I am writing using a process or simply 'going for it' in an unstructured way. That is, I need to be in a mood to write, and to want to write, or if not want to, then to feel some kind of compulsion or emotional need to create. I don't mean to be pretentious about it, but it happens. A subject or concern has usually been fluttering around in my mind for several days, perhaps sparked by a particular image, someone else's writing, a painting, anything that strikes me, and it gradually evolves into something more concrete – a few lines or phrases, sometimes more, occasionally a whole paragraph or verse, or an idea of a way to work. I usually write with pen on paper, work up several drafts within a few days and then get it onto the computer. It will be read, re-read, worked and reworked over the next six months before I decide it is finished. Once I do decide that it will stay on my desk for a week or so until I am absolutely convinced it really is finished. Then, that's it. I don't endlessly tweak and prune after that – it gets submitted to magazines etc. and lives its life out in the world. Or, it may end up simply in my file as a finished piece of work I don't rate very highly.

Are you prolific? How often do you write?

I regard myself as very unprolific, with often months between poems. But when I am writing I often seem to write a sequence or series, at least a group of poems. I know I have a reputation for being prolific. However, I may just be good at getting my work published! I'm also someone who is quite suspicious of authors who only write 25 poems in two years, ready for their 'slim volume' of new work. Writers write, that's what they do. If you engage with writing (that is, by reading other authors, magazines, critical work, anything), it seems unlikely to me that a writer doesn't write for that long; or if you get blank spells, which we all do, that you won't bounce back and create a number of works or a longer work later on. Of course, it's possible these slim-volume poets are just brutal self-editors.

What important influences have shaped your current interest? What are you reading at the moment?

Certainly discussions with yourself (as per the excerpt 'From a Correspondence' published in *Acumen* magazine) and others like Tony Lopez and Phil Terry in

Exeter have changed the way I look at poetry. As do on-going debates with other editors, friends and authors such as Brian Pearce, Clark Allison and William Oxley – though we often disagree about many things! I also have long-standing correspondences with several people around the world, often by e-mail, many of which have opened my eyes to new writers and possibilities in writing. The linguistically-innovative stuff around at the moment has certainly made me sit up and look at lots of new work, and think about how language works, but I am still drawn towards a kind of modernist (rather than postmodernist) way of writing – I still err towards ideas of self-expression and experimentation, although one very much in flux and able to draw on everything that has gone before (not necessarily ironically), often resisting closure. More and more I find music, particularly free jazz and contemporary classical, informs my writing as much as other writing, although I read a lot of fiction. But ideas of tonal centres, repetitive beats, slabs of sound, offer ways to work with themes and motifs within poetry. John Coltrane, Miles Davis, Takemitsu and John Cage have a lot to answer for!

A look along my reading shelf: a history of jazz-rock, biographies of Patti Smith and David Sylvian, Kodwo Eshun's *More Brilliant Than The Sun*, poetry books by Hayden Carruth, Barrett Watten, Michael Ondaatje and Jorie Graham, Charles Olson's *Selected Writings*, Dubravka Ugresic's novel and essays, *The Sandman Dust Covers* by Dave Mckean, *Hiding* by Mark C Taylor, and others. Waiting on the 'to read' shelf are books by Clark Coolidge, Greg Egan, Don Cupitt and Sadie Plant. This morning I bought Salman Rushdie's BFI book on *The Wizard of Oz*, Peter Childs' *the twentieth century in poetry: a critical survey*, and Joseph M. Conte's *Unending Design*. A hand-printed chapbook and CD of a reading by William Everson arrived in the mail this morning from America.

Are you interested in hybridizing poetries, or hybridizing poetry with other art forms?

Yes, when it wants to happen. As a painter, I know paintings don't need language – all too often collaborations simply explain themselves too much. Having said that I do work with artists, musicians and other writers from time to time. I certainly believe all art forms seem to have communal underlying ways of doing things, mutual concerns, many similarities. Rhythm, shaping, formal ideas and concepts, line… these seem to be applicable to many art forms.

In what ways do these other art forms inform & influence your work?

These other art forms are usually an inspiration or spring board for my writing, or my painting. My prose poem *Shadow Triptych* came out of a visit to the

Francis Bacon exhibition at the Hayward last year. That visit, and the process of writing afterwards, raised some questions I wanted to try and work through – questions about paint itself, art galleries and the fashion/reputation end of fine art, faith and doubt, etc. So it was a starting point, although some actual images/ events from my visit to the exhibition – either the paintings themselves or my impression of other visitors there – remain in the text. It inspired me to create, using a collage system. Often, of course, influences will be far more subtle and indirect than this, from the way music may alter the ambience of my study to a long-lasting effect of reading or seeing something.

Have you collaborated with other artists or writers on any work recently? How has this developed your poetry?

I sent some monoprints to Sheila Murphy who responded to them in writing… Sheila is always a delight to work with. Trombone Press did a pamphlet. I am working (separately) with two other visual artists, Robert Garlitz and Bruce Bitmead, on collaborative paintings – we are both starting paintings which the other will finish. Ray Malone and I recently worked on *An Undestroyable Hush*, published by Apparitions Press – he drew to my prose-poem; I designed the booklet. I guess this is a more traditional collaboration, and could be seen as merely illustrating. Bob Garlitz and I regularly use each other's e-mails to cut-up into new poems we are working on. I owe my friend Morgan Bryan some tapes of excerpts from my *Stone Angels* prose collection he wanted to work into his ambient music project.

How do you select work for a poetry list/anthology? Should poetry lists/ anthologies demonstrate consistency, or diversity?

I believe once a concept is worked out for an anthology – be it a broad overview, a gender bias, or a particular critical viewpoint – the anthologiser will know who they want to include. I find 'open' briefs, with less writers (and more of each of their work) far more interesting than sprawling one-poem-per-author projects. As for poetry lists, let it be the editor's decision. But let them stop pretending that only their list is worth reading and that there are no other types of poetry. Let's put an end to 'future of poetry' blurbs and simply offer it to the reader as something we are interested in.

With Stride I get more and more open to many types of writing, but tougher and tougher within each of the types of poetry I publish. I'm all for diversity and have never understood why people couldn't listen to all sorts of music or look at all types of painting. Eventually, you realise they aren't interested in, and don't understand, how music or painting works, that they are listening to 'tunes' or looking at 'images'… I am interested in words as poetry and fiction (and the hybrids in between) – interested in a way that allows me to read many types of work. It doesn't, of course, mean any of us will, or indeed should, like it all.

Is there a 'new poetry'? What is it?

No, there isn't. There is simply a big group of mediocre writers being marketed well, often in an exciting way with snazzy covers and snappy quotes. I don't mind them being sold at all – to repeat myself, it's the bullshit and hype that goes with it I hate. And people who should know better taking it seriously.

Does good poetry sell, or popular poetry? Does popular really mean good?

Very little poetry sells full stop. A few very well accepted authors like Larkin and Hughes sell well, popular performance poets like Roger McGough sell well, and doggerel like Pam Ayres sells even better, of course. Below these big sellers there are genuinely popular poets like Carol Ann Duffy who also sell, but not in the way those I've just mentioned do. But we all know that most poetry books sell less than 1,000 copies, especially individual author's volumes, and particularly books by new authors. That's not popular; popular usually means a few good reviews in the major newspapers and poetry magazines.

Like all art forms, poetry will take a good while to shake down to its lasting canon, even longer to well and truly settle. Look at the way authors like David Jones and W.S. Graham have been regarded in the last 20 years, who knows what will happen to the current crop? Look at the way Dylan Thomas hardly gets a look in now. I think John Burnside and Carol Ann Duffy will outstay any New Gen nonsense, but looking at the recent Penguin and Picador anthologies I sincerely hope the poets that will last from the 1960s on are not the ones currently offered to us. It's all a bit 'emperor's new clothes' I feel – very few people are prepared to point out that there's nothing there, to voice dissent (although I was pleased to see a very negative *Agenda* review of the Penguin anthology). There was a moment a while back when *Conductors of Chaos* was published, and Iain Sinclair's novels and prose-poems were being reissued and being reviewed/featured in the nationals, and other things seemed to be bubbling up, that I thought something was going to change. It all seems to have disappeared again with millenium fever taking over.

I want to see the likes of Tom Raworth and Robert Creeley mentioned more often; John Riley, Robert Lax, David Miller, Alan Halsey, Gavin Selerie given the attention their work deserves; William Everson and Kenneth Patchen critically reconsidered and contextualised. But maybe it doesn't matter? Maybe, without being all 60s about it, poetry is intrinsically small-scale and revolutionary, and has a small audience? Maybe it only stops being 'subversive' many years later, and we don't want it appropriated and neutered too fast?

Is contemporary poetry a divided thing? Divided which ways? How are you bridging the gaps?

It's very divided. Into camps of people who somehow think their way of working, their type of poetry (and often simply their own poetry) is the only way you can work. Into groups of people who deny the validity of, say, making people laugh at a poem in the pub, or helping someone through their grieving with a poem. Into groups of academics who want to discuss poetry within the formal constraints of academic argument with all its footnotes and nods to previous academics. Into groups of creative writing workshop poets who refuse to consider anything they don't like, or don't easily understand. Into groups of self-help mutual back-patters who wouldn't dream of criticising anyone, and who think poetry is about being 'nice' and 'polite', preferably with end-of-line rhymes as well. Into groups of people who don't seem to understand that all sorts of poetry use the same language and are rooted in the same ways of writing, shares the same past, draws on the same poetic history. It is the attitudes and schools/cliques which divide poetry, not the writers and their writing.

I have been involved in poetry group discussion on the net where people quite seriously write that Faber has never published a good poetry book. You ask them about Eliot or WS Graham and you get shrugged off. You criticise the speed at which Tom Raworth reads at and you find yourself dismissed as someone who doesn't like contemporary poetry!

I think it is perfectly acceptable, indeed desirable, to use poetry for many things – relaxation, humour, performance, experimentation, linguistic exploration (although I draw the line at polemic!). I believe we need an openness and honesty towards all types of poetry. Not by diluting our poetry but by entering both academic and non-academic debates as best you can.

For myself, I have chosen to write letters and to take on the Reviews Editorship of *Orbis*. Being able to review Iain Sinclair, or Lee Harwood in *Orbis* is small way of bridging some divides – but those reviews have to be in plain English and relate to the sorts of poetry *Orbis* readers already read. That strikes me as a very necessary and important thing to do.

Stride continues to publish a wide array of poetries, types of poetry, and to contextualise them (and our music and fiction books) with a series of 'Conversation Pieces' and 'Research Documents'. The latter includes books of essays and reviews.

I know I am not alone in wanting change – I can see an openness in the editorial decisions of many small press publishing houses, and also in Carcanet, particularly, who I now regard as the best of the major poetry publishers. People like John Kinsella are able to navigate many types of poetry, with the added advantage of being outside the UK clique systems. I hope to see this kind of openness and willingness to exchange ideas, discuss all types of poetry, and desire to communicate, blossom in the next century. Change and flux are energising and life-affirming, not something to be scared of.

David Morley

Here is one story about editing: I have two roles as an editor, both of which I regard as seamless with writing poetry. The first as an editor of anthologies; the second as an editor for Arc Publications where I look after the British and Irish poetry lists. I am very conscious that my role at Arc over the past seven years is an inheritance. It was Tony Ward's pioneering work from the seventies onwards that created the frame and ethos of the company. Although I am at times tempted to set up my own publishing house, I still find myself completely in sympathy with Ward's vision, so this is his story too.

Arc Publications is above all a team; the manuscripts we publish pass through a number of hands before they settle within our list. The tale needs telling of how this engaging company came about and why. The fact that our editorial decisions are made collectively contrasts with the editorial process at presses such as Bloodaxe, Carcanet, Anvil and Enitharmon. It was not always so. Tony Ward, now Arc's general editor, took over the precursor of this firm in 1969 from a writers' collective based in the Medway Towns 'because they edited by committee and so nothing was produced'.[1] Six pamphlets later, Tony was running the press solo. His catholic editing picked up Bob Cobbing, Thomas A. Clark and Ken Smith's collection of prose poems *Frontwards in a Backwards Movie*. He then entered into a partnership with the Arvon Foundation at Lumb Bank. Later, he acquired his own printing equipment, and moved the outfit into a mill near Hebden Bridge: 'the important thing is that Arc printed its own books; I had total control over production, and this continues to be a deciding factor for writers who want to be published by us'. His editorial percipience included work by Benjamin Peret, Jeff Nuttall and Bill Griffiths. The authors enjoyed high production values; Arc's role as a printer in the 1970s recalls the time of the fine and adventurous editions of Virginia and Leonard Woolf's Hogarth Press after the First World War.

Ward's remit specifically embraced printing for small presses. That role broadened after he parted company with Arvon and developed a funding relationship with the then Yorkshire Arts, printing some of the output from Anvil, Galloping Dog Press, Ferry Press, Spectacular Diseases and Trigram. 'It introduced me to writers I wouldn't have otherwise read such as the poets of *The English Intelligencer* like Denise Riley, Jeremy Prynne, John Riley and Douglas Oliver. John Riley's versions of Osip Mandelstam were a particular revelation'. Ward went on to publish new books from the Intelligencer pantheon, including small collections by Michael Grant, Peter Riley and David Chaloner: 'It was a question of whether I believed it was important poetry or not. For example, I didn't really respond to Peret's poetry but I knew it was important to publish it. Unfortunately for all concerned with new writing, Charles Osborne, the self-styled scourge of literature and the small press world, was then appointed Director of Literature at The Arts Council'. Osborne's anti-artistic bent is documented in his insolent and badly-written autobiography. His bungling still affects the Literature Department's allocation to this day. Despite these cuts, one of the hallmarks of Arc books is that they continued to be sublimely printed. Collectors items included D.M. Thomas's *News from the Front* and the Ivor Cutler series of books which are the size of a cream-cracker and which sell like hot cakes ('He came to us because nobody else would produce his books the way he wanted them'). But business was still a struggle despite helpful associations with Graham Mort's Giant Steps Press and John Killick's Littlewood. Building a new editorial board in 1993 revived the press: 'I found it hugely advantageous. It gave a better qualified judgement overall, and access to a bigger spread of poets'.

This is where I re-enter this story. Ward's co-editors were now Michael Hulse and myself. We re-launched the press with both an International and UK Series. With solid new collections from Rose Ausländer, Jackie Wills, W.N. Herbert, John Hartley Williams and Don Atkinson, our intention was to choose the best of what came in through the post, but I also actively commissioned poets whose work we admired from their appearances in magazines. Hulse pushed us striking collections from Robert Gray and John Kinsella (Australia), C.K. Stead and Dinah Hawken (New Zealand), Tomaz Saluman (Slovenia) and Don Coles (Canada). What we didn't make in sales we made up in goodwill: suddenly good British poets started offering us work we could publish, notably James Sutherland-Smith, Andy Brown and Glyn Maxwell (his verse-drama *Wolfpit*). Michael Hulse moved on to start his own publishing house, Leviathan, and to take up the editorial reins of *Stand* with John Kinsella. We expanded the board to include Kinsella himself and Robert Gray, and appointed Jean Boase-Beier to lead up a new Translation Series. This has built a vigorous, collegial editorial that – unlike the earlier Medway adventure – now makes bold decisions with shared responsibility. Our funding is paltry – none of us receives a *sou* for what we do – but none of us are in the literature business to make a comfortable living. For myself, I can review my progress as a writer by what I choose to publish by other people. The micro-editing of an author's book feeds back on my own work; it makes me intensely self-critical and is one of the reasons I haven't published many poems in Britain since 1997. The downside of my job is the slush-pile. We may well receive fine collections out of the blue but, as with other presses, the majority of what arrives unsolicited is poorly-written and sometimes freakishly presented.

What are your interests regarding questions of sexual politics and gender in poetry? How do you feel about Women's Anthologies and the arguments surrounding recent ones?

I'm not behind the proposition that there should be more anthologies of contemporary poetry by women. I think the moment has passed, and I mean *moment*. Not one single woman student I've taught thinks well of the more recent women's anthologies. They find the editorial rationale patronising and alienating. They agree with Sheenagh Pugh's plea to: '...stop producing anthologies that suggest there were two species, rather than two genders, writing in the late twentieth century'.[2] In contrast, I am very much behind the project for more anthologies of, say, pre-Modernist poetry by women and welcomed Bloodaxe's *Classical Women Poets* translated and edited by Josephine Balmer. A number of friends and colleagues at Warwick – the novelist Jane Stevenson, the poet Peter Davidson, and Germaine Greer – are working on an enormous anthology *The Oxford Book of Early Modern Women Poets*. Jane is also discovering numerous classical women poets writing in Latin from antiquity to the eighteenth century, unearthing verses and emblems from libraries spread around the world. It's detective work, with a strong socio-political stripe. I've witnessed the research and read the proofs; these projects are an absolutely breathtaking reclamation: the social-poetic equivalent of poldering the North Sea from Hull to Rotterdam. They seem to me to be urgent projects; they give a much more forbearing and generous 'take' on notions of sisterhood than any contemporary anthology of women's poetry. What is striking about these newly-discovered women poets is that they are notable for their successes, and that they were integrated and valued in their communities. If observers are honestly alert to marginalisation and questions of value, maybe they should take their bearings and readings from the 'missing' women poets: that is, the 'missing in action'.

What are your interests re: politics in poetry?

At best, contemporary poems grounded in social and political issues can be incredibly moving, honest and timeless. Two powerful examples arose from the Gulf War: Michael Hulse's 'Mother of Battles' (Arc Publications) and Jo Shapcott's 'Phrase Book' (Oxford University Press). I also admire Tony Conran's 'Elegy for the Welsh Dead in the Falkland Islands, 1982' from *Blodeuwedd* (Poetry Wales Press). Why do these three poems succeed when others do not? Possibly because their focus is as much on language as on subject – Hulse's on mythological address, Shapcott's on newsspeak, Conran's on Welsh verse strategy. Poets who appear to *deliberate* over such subjects – and a number of good English poets appear unable to stop themselves – produce verses that come over as opportunistic and ugly in their manipulativeness. There are so many under-analysed poems about Kosovo and Belfast. I surmise that is what the 'contemporary poetry audience' is supposed to want to read. As an editor and writer, as a person, I disagree. Maybe some think it is poetry's function to dip its pen into other people's guts, so long as the dead and dying are foreign but recognisably European. Iain Sinclair calls this verse, rightly I think, 'a substitute for those black-bordered sentimental Victorian verses, invented to appease the demons of tragedy'. It is a problem, a very English problem. I am personally very suspicious of it. Maybe I am too close to it as an editor. Sometimes I feel I am watching a series of repeats, or supernumerary episodes from a series I once liked when I was adolescent.

What's going on in contemporary poetry that interests you? Is poetry in a healthy state or is it heading nowhere?

So what have been the ructions that recent anthologies have tracked well and that have influenced the way I write? *Life Studies* was defining for more than one generation, as were other Transatlantic fertilisations – The New York School, the various L=A=N=G=U=A=G=E projects, Black Mountain, the Objectivists... (I feel strongly that Charles Tomlinson, Jonathan Williams and Gael Turnbull deserve medals for assisting these fertilisations.) Of late, probably the most active influence on the syntax and diction of British poetry comes from Australia and New Zealand – Les Murray, John Tranter, John Kinsella, Geoffery Lehmann, Dinah Hawken, Allen Curnow and the late James Baxter – and also from Canada in the poetry of Michael Ondaatje, Ann Michaels, Margaret Atwood and Don Coles. The strategies of a number of Irish poets, namely Derek Mahon, Seamus Heaney, and Paul Muldoon have been welcomed and adopted by many British poets in the nineties.

I don't have space to enumerate the many and constructive impacts of these and other poets and projects on new British poetry. I would say that were we to construct a new anthology of poetry and poetics, it's not the metaphors of cartography or seismography you would need but a real spinning globe with real pins stuck in it. The sites of composition, publication, distribution and reception contain living poets who are also editors. A great many of these people talk to one another, read one another, publish one another and review one another. They are activists. It's an earth-sized version of the 'map' of the British-Cambridge Avant-Garde that Iain Sinclair talks up in his Introduction to the anthology *Conductors of Chaos* (a club of poets that can now be considered part of the mainstream). The world has become very small; the ease of information-transfer defies any poet to remain ignorant of what is going in the next town or next country. There is no next country in 'world poetry', indeed little connection between the place of authorship and those of distribution and consumption.

Are you interested in hybridising poetries, or hybridising poetry with other art forms? In what ways do these other art forms inform and influence your work? Have you collaborated with other artists or writers on any work recently?

I see collaboration as a liberation because in general it means more constrictions are placed on my working methods. I find any constriction (say, in form) emancipating: 'Whatever diminishes constraint diminishes strength. The more constraints one imposes, the more one frees one's self of the chains that shackle the spirit' – Igor Stravinsky. Two years ago, the Scottish sculptor David Annand created twin models of dancers (designed from studying video of a contemporary dance company). These 'Two Graces' were each mounted on three-metre stainless steel triple-helices. My commission (shall we call it a poem?) had to weave down the helices – thus, one twisting line per helix.[3] Obviously, every line should be read as the first, second or third line of a poem (chickenfeed I know compared to Raymond Queneau's *Cent mille milliards de poèmes*). I had spatial constriction to contend with: each line needed to have thirty-three characters (including spaces). Apart from spatial restriction, three-dimensionality, and continuity between lines, there were the very intriguing factors that people would read this poem daily; that it would be in a very public and busy space (in this case near Blackpool's Tower, that talismanic phallus of my entire childhood in that town); that Annand wanted at least 'a dozen different versions before going for the final' (the poem as a 'maquette'); that it would be written on to the sculpture using a metal-punch (therefore the poem could be read by touch) so no Q's were allowed (don't ask me why); that the poem had to reflect the visual concept of the sculptor's theme; and that the deadline was one week. This kind of commission is a force-field of demands disguised as expectations. The gravity of these demands meant I worked more swiftly, and thought even more laterally than usual. I also found the idea of such a *public*-ation raising the stakes: it made me write better and more clearly because I knew there was to be a big, largely non-poetry reading audience. And, I should point out, clarity did not necessarily lead to accessibility. The finished poem was a readable, palimpsestic act of Chinoiserie.

The parameters I'm working with now are the size of a city – Coventry . I'm embarked on a two-year commission with the French artist Françoise Schein and the German poet/sculptor Jochen Gerz to reinvent Coventry City centre. Coventry was bombed to char in November 1940 by the Luftwaffe, and 're-bombed' by spiritless planning and design in the Harold Macmillan era (an exception to the ferro-concrete being Basil Spence's new cathedral). I regard my collaborators as writers. Conversely, they regard me as an artisan like themselves. Françoise's key work to my mind is *Inscrever Os Direitos Do Homen*: the renovation/recreation of La Station Parque (part of La Mètro de Lisbonne) as a text-based sculpture composed entirely of polylingual versions of the United Nations Charter for Human Rights. Jochen Gerz is well-known for his 'disappearing sculptures': obelisks and memorials embroidered with personal opinions, even naked prejudices, inscribed directly by citizens of the city in which the sculpture stands (and which then disappears into the earth). Both artists attempt to produce very high-calibre, cutting edge work, that is underpinned by a humanistic philosophy, and that is created in a writer's partnership with the people who then have to live with the artistic result. Much British public art doesn't seem to embrace those ambitions, although matters are improving as more architects and artists work with more people, including poets.

I relish the democracy of collaborating with such painters, sculptors and video-makers. Their outlook is refreshing in that they rarely seem to embrace a hieratic view of their role as an artist, and are more engaged by a spirit of working in an artistic community (something Frank O'Hara noticed in his dealings with New York painters). Maybe I am lucky in my co-workers, or maybe I preserve the perspective of being an outsider scientist-now-academic, a quality I hope I exercise as an editor. But there seems a greater security about what we might call production values and artistic standards than that which I find among some young poets. Some of them seem as fiercely competitive as scorpions fighting in a corpse.

The notion of 'working poet' may seem to some an oxymoron, but that view is a very English perception.[4] Let me illustrate this by an anecdote. On a recent lecture tour of China I was taken by my genial neo-Capitalistic hosts to the Guangzhou Museum of Modern Culture, a former Buddhist monastery that, at the height of Mao's Cultural Revolution, cunningly disguised itself as a printing factory to survive the vandalism of the Red Guards (they printed the *Little Red Book* for good measure). I was shown the exhibits. The exquisitely elaborate paper cuttings, for example, were for sale at rice-bowl prices, and the woman cutting them in front of you had taken five years to learn this art. The young man dressed in his Red Army uniform was painfully executing a micro-portrait of jungle fauna on the inside wall of a bottle, the mouth of which was barely wide enough to take his toothpick-sized brush. He had trained for seven years to do this. Next we came to the bone-carvers, their bone-spheres interiorly and exteriorly hand-etched into eleven moving globes, each globe independent in their motion and yet still one sphere. It takes a carver thirty years to learn this. 'These people', I said to my hosts, 'they are Great Artists. Are they famous in

China?'. The rapid, laughing answer punctured me: 'Not at all. These are not artists and this is not art. If these working folk are artists then China has factories of artists. This...', my host grinned, holding up one sphere of fifteen independent parts, 'is *work*. What you might 'do for a life'. Craft, not art'. What, I thought to myself, would this man make of our English poets?

In what way does a project of this scale inform and influence your work?

Firstly, it informs and influences my philosophy. For example, I would affirm that in literature, things can be said in words, or by means of other arts, or by means of a building. I place my editing work at Arc and my role at Warwick University within the same philosophy. But this is a hard matter to get across in England! That a poet, if they're going to be a poet, should make any project cause for poetry. That a poet on a good day could run ICI, create a new university or a wonderful, thriving business – and that they could call these physical projects poems in themselves because they are using their talent and vocation with language to produce and run them. Neil Astley's Bloodaxe and Michael Schmidt's Carcanet are respectively the modern day's *Iliad* and *Odyssey* in the form of good businesses. Arc is more of an *Arcadia*: a zone of gladiatorial rhetoric. Just because these projects are not stanza-shaped words in a slim volume does not mean that they are not a species of poetry, a sister to 'composition'.

Here's a corollary to this thesis. I greatly admire Ian Hamilton Finlay's 'Hellenisation Plan' for his garden at Stonypath (Stonypath was subsequently named Little Sparta). The garden-as-poem concept has a fine, maverick tradition with poets such as Pope and Shenstone judged 'as social thinkers distilling ethical values from the transformation of their landscape'.[5] The role of gardener was assumed by poets who seek 'a place to stand'. A poet working so closely with an organic, natural medium produces a counter-order: its inherent 'poem'. Now, I wouldn't go so far as Finlay's playful 'Garden centres must become the Jacobin Clubs of the new Revolution',[6] but I see nothing artificial or compromising to poetry about recreating a city as a poem, or even my conceptualising Coventry as a *tabula rasa* for my writing. It's both a civic and compositional activity, and I will bomb my poems gently so that they are natural to that city's soil. Finlay – 'Gardening activity is of five kinds, namely sowing, planting, fixing, placing, maintaining. In so far as gardening is an Art, all these may be taken under the one head, composing'.

Secondly, such collaborative commissioned work makes me write poems and sequences I would not have written otherwise. I should never have dreamed of re-writing The Coventry Carols nor re-inventing the mediaeval *Ludus Coventriae* [the Coventry Mystery Plays] unless someone gave me the deadline, the money and the audience. I feel the whole idea of the commission is one poets should encourage. Paul Muldoon recently described university writing programmes as the 'new patrons' for writers.[7] To an extent that's true and British universities need not make the mistakes of their American counterparts. Civic authorities and publishers can join universities in that role We need to revive and encourage the concept of patronage.

How has cross-art form collaboration developed your poetry?

Firstly, it prevents me worrying in the narrow hours about the nature of inspiration. Secondly, it makes me write with a cartographer's spirit of scale that has nothing to do with my egotism, and more to do with Iain Sinclair's strategies in *Lights Out for the Territory* – namely 'mapping'. You must try and perceive your work 'from the air'. The overall code of the commissioned poems must have that bird's eye perception behind their combination and placing, like walking the plot of *Ulysses* and thus super-imposing the shape of a question-mark on the street-map of Dublin. It's not unlike editing. The poem(s) must map and plot the place you are working on, as though you are drawing a city on to a page then splicing those pages into a book. Bruce Chatwin's: '. . . Songlines stretching across the continents and ages; that wherever men have trodden they have left a trail of song...' is a beautiful poetic and anthropological concept that appeals to me. It's a useful paradigm for my notion of a city as an open book, one already written by its history – its 'palace of memory' – and one waiting to be written. Recall Thom Gunn's 'A Map of the City': *By the recurrent lights I see / Endless potentiality, / The crowded, broken, and unfinished! / I would not have the risk diminished.*

NOTES

1 From an interview with Tony Ward, July 5th 1999
2 'Women's Issues', *Thumbscrew* 8, Summer 1997, p. 22
3 I learned about the possibility of twisting a line physically through studying hypertext Chinese poems that Wellsweep Press placed on the World Wide Web in, I think, 1995. Also, Jack Prelutsky's children's poetry CDROM, *Forty Performing Bananas*, gave me a ludic enough starting point: as with many children's poetry CDROMs, the lines in a poem can be made to dance and swerve.
4 When I use 'English' or 'England' in this piece, I mean what the words mean.
5 Ian Hamilton Finlay: *A Visual Primer by Yves Abrioux*, Reaktion Books 1985
6 From Finlay's 'Unconnected Sentences on Gardening'
7 At 'The Needs of Writers' conference, Warwick University Writing Programme, May 1998.

Maggie O'Sullivan

What's going on in contemporary poetry that interests you? Is poetry in a healthy state at the moment or is it heading nowhere?

An extraordinary range of exciting, poetries and poetic practises have recently been made available through the appearance of a number of crucial anthologies – *Out Of Everywhere: linguistically innovative poetry by women in North America & the UK*; *From the Other Side of the Century*; *Poems for the Millenium* (2 vols) and *Word Score Utterance Choreography*. Particularly pertinent to these isles are *Conductors of Chaos* and *Other: British and Irish Poetry Since 1970*. These anthologies demonstrate, that despite mainstream omission and indifference or lip-service, there exists a substantial body of significant, challenging work by women and men who engage in explorative, formally progressive strategies and processual language practises which forms an explosive counterpoint to the canonical static picture of our time. In its volume and seriousness of poetic practise, this work is equal to, yet almost totally separate from, the dominant body of poetry that the controlling UK cultural industries acknowledge and promote.

These, together with small press independent journals and magazines, committed to formally progressive work, mainly from the US and Canada but also in the UK and Ireland: France (*Gare du Nord*): Australia (*Boxkite*), and the few dynamic UK small presses at the forefront of publishing international progressive writing – Sound & Language, writers forum, etruscan books and Reality Street Editions – to name a few – whose valiant uncompromising efforts have succeeded in bringing out some of the most exciting work currently being done within the innovative and modernist traditions.

Also, the wealth of recently published essay collections / critical works such as Charles Bernstein's *Close Listening: Poetry and the Performed Word*; Marjorie Perloff's *Poetry On and Off the Page* and Keith Tuma's *Fishing by Obstinate Isles: Modern and Postmodern British Poetry and American Readers* open some windows on what is currently happening outside of the closure of the mainstream. And then there's the Buffalo Electronic Poetry Centre... and the internet... etc.

Unfortunately, the majority of the small press progressive work cannot be obtained through your average bookshop and this I consider to be a deeply pernicious state. To gain access to anything other than standard off-the-shelves stuff means mail order. Most of us who are interested/involved in this work know of the channels for access. However, the difficulty is in locating / accessing potential readers/writers through the standard outlets.

As far as what I call the mainstream poetry is concerned, it is static and closed when mediocre versifiers are exclusively promoted and championed by the media. The message is either write this way or that way (mostly there's not even a choice, it's write this way and you will succeed, i.e. become 'one of our leading poets' winning bursaries, prizes, awards, etc.) or it's get lost.

However, what keeps me going is access to and celebration of work I cannot live without and it's at large in the vast area of hybridisation, contradiction, multidimensionality and multivocality, beyond all the getting-on & display & monuments where all such exciting work is taking place. One either needs (as nourishment) this or not. Because needing it, saying 'yes,' – as many yesses as in Molly Bloom's soliloquy – is to refuse to buy into the institutional closure of the mainstream's lying promotional assaults.

What important influences have shaped your current interests? What are you reading at present?

Moving out of London. Living beside animals. Frogs. Country night skies. Intimacy/Connection with Cats. My father who was born and brought up barefoot on an earth floor in the stone house his father built, outside of Skibbereen, West Cork. A sense of the ancestral self. Finnegan's Wake. Irish music, culture. Jerome Rothenberg's brilliant anthologies. The work of Kurt Schwitters, Beckett, Artaud, Joseph Beuys, Nancy Spero, Bill Griffiths, Erin Mouré, Prospero Saez, Cecelia Vicuna, Susan Howe. I'm encountering/re-encountering and enjoying Paul Celan, Jackson Mac Low, Michael Palmer, Johanna Drucker, Daphne Marlatt, Alice Notley, Lesley Scalapino, Catherine Walsh, Sarah Murphy's extraordinary fictions, Nathaniel Mackey's *Discrepant Engagement – Dissonance, Cross-Culturality & Experimental Writing*, Bruce Andrews' *Paradise & Method: Poetics & Praxis*, Paul Carter's *The Lie Of The Land* and *Living Water* by Olof Alexandersson.

Hybrids & Collaborations?

I collaborated with Bruce Andrews on *Excla*, which Writers Forum published in 1993. This collaboration was an exciting, challenging one. We did all the work via mail – working/reading through each other's work and responding to the vocabulary, lexical and thematic tints, commenting, responding, twisting, reversing, collaging etc., until we each came up with about 3000 handwritten words on tiny pieces of paper, which formed the basis of our eventual collaboration. Working with on-going material input from another and thus being stretched to new procedures and approaches was energising and exhilarating. While the collaboration, which took about 2 years was in process, it encouraged me to a greater fluency and took me into what I might call more collaging and contradictioning practises.

Also, on a purely pragmatic level, receiving the package from Bruce and knowing he'd be waiting for one in return was a focus and motivating factor. It was a liberating experience.

How do you select work for a poetry list / anthology? Should poetry lists / anthologies demonstrate consistency, or diversity?

At the invitation of Ken Edwards and Wendy Mulford (Reality Street Editions) who wanted to produce an anthology to reflect the astonishing work by women who broadly speaking, are working with language - at the leading edge of innovative poetics – I selected the work of 30 poets for *Out of Everywhere* to show that much of the formally progressive and significant work over recent years, particularly in the US, is being made by women.

Each poet I selected engages in explorative, formally progressive language practises which go beyond the confines of representation and transparency or the ubiquitous realist / confessional reductionist mode and each in her own way takes great risks and commits herself to excavating language in all its multiple voices and tongues, known and unknown.

Consequently, many of them, through brave insistence and engagement in explorative, formally progressive language practises, find themselves excluded from conventional, explicitly generically committed or thematic anthologies of women's poetry. I think the diversity, breadth, and range of visual and linguistic attention of their different practises is extraordinary, as is their willingness to explore larger, cultural, social and philosophical perspectives and also engage with long poetic sequences or in project-orientated work. This engagement with larger poetic discourses and practises embraces inter and multi-media work and performative practises.

Should poetry be difficult, or should poets make their work easily understandable?

Divisory terms such as 'difficult' and 'understandable' are examples of the conformist rhetoric of the UK literary establishment which is built on stasis and closure – standardised to the utmost degree to accommodate prevailing establishment protocols – where writing is a window that imitates, reproduces, captures the world as it exists. Such terms are irrelevant to poetry which is fundamentally a practise of liberty and not contingent upon subordination to the linguistic or perceptual static absolutes of a product-peddling culture.

The writer's responsibility is not to an ulterior authority but to the experience, excavation and revelation of the work itself. Imagination and vision are not subordinate to social/political or cultural constraints.

D. H. Lawrence in *Chaos in Poetry* talks (and I gist him blunderingly) about the difficulty the poet faces in having to confront, not only a blank page but a page already so covered with pre-existing, pre-established cliches, conventions, opinions and explanation that it is first necessary to erase, even to shred and destroy, to rent the firmament so as to be able to begin.

Why do some poets choose to operate from within the small press only?

If it weren't for the tiny handful of editors of small presses who have supported and valued my work and made it available, to the best of their means, over the decades, I probably wouldn't have been published at all and you might never have heard of my work and wouldn't be now inviting me to contribute to this project.

Each of my works – which explore visual/textual/spatial processes, addressing/ contouring the infinite site/sight of the page in terms of structural, notational, kinetic & assemblative values, etc., always with the focus on the materiality of language: I simply don't think or work in lines – demand new formal and aesthetic considerations in terms of overall presentation.

As it's the poetics of the long or project-orientated work that most compels and preoccupies me – not least because of the depth & range of textual, aesthetic terrains and attentions required by both myself and reader/hearer, each of my books tends to be a single long work so the presentation of a work in published form is an extension of the CONSTRUCTING/FIGURING OUT processes at large within the work and take in the formal aesthetics of book as text, as artefact, performance. In the case of my current project – *her/story:eye* – I envisage it will be presented over time as a series of works through a series of various books.

The editors of the small presses who have made my books have ensured that the physical presence of each work in printed form has always been true to the text's integrity. In short, they have allowed each work its own breath. By its nature, small press printing/publishing can allow for variances, idiosyncrasies, originalities & vitalities to be borne forth without confinement or constraint to make a work subordinate to the prevailing culturally sanctioned package of the slim volume of accommodatory verse.

What is the point of an anthology?

The aim behind *Out of Everywhere* is to demonstrate via a sampling showcase of 30 women, that some of the most challenging, linguistically innovative poetry over recent years is being made by women and that although the majority of the poets featured in *OOE*, through engagement in explorative, formally progressive language practises, find themselves usually excluded from 'women's canons', such work does, however, connect up with innovative writing practises by men.

Editing *OOE* was rewarding and enriching. As well as giving me the opportunity of working closely with writing by poets I admire and who had contributed to my own development over the years: it also provided an opportunity to present the work of new, young poets. I had difficulty selecting 30 poets because the whole point of *OOE* is to highlight the fact there is such a wealth of radical, innovative work out there by women and also to suggest to the (particularly new) reader/writer directions for further potential areas of richness and discovery.

I hope that the presence of *OOE*, as both a vibrant celebration and a vital resource, will in some small way, have a long range effect in subverting and rupturing the literary mainstream's denial of such adventurous, intellectually challenging and imaginative work.

For Ken Edwards, Wendy Mulford and myself, the publication of *OOE* represents a project to both celebrate and make as available as possible to new readers/writers, the writing we passionately believe in.

What social & political interests motivate your work, if any?

My background undoubtedly has shaped who I am / how I am in the world / my work. My father and mother had little schooling and my father worked as a labourer in and out of work all his life. We were brought up on the edge, locked out, without any voice.

As well as the materiality, the primacy of language, that most preoccupies me, in what can be done underneath, behind, with-in the multidimensionality that is language, my work is driven by the spoken, sounded or breathing voice. Particularly I have always been haunted by issues of VOICELESSNESS – inarticulacy – silence – soundlessness – breathlessness – how are soundings or voices that are other-than or invisible or dimmed or marginalised or excluded or without privilege, or locked out, made UNofficial, reduced by ascendant systems of centrality and closure, configured or Sounded or given form & potency: how can I body forth or configure such sounds, such tongues, such languages, such muteness, such multivocality, such error – & this is perhaps why the non-vocal in mark & the non-word in sound or language – make up much of the fabrics & structures of my own compositions.

Working with the lexicon – whether regular, pre-existing or newly-made – mis-spelt, mis-heard, mis-read, compound – contraction or part of a word such as a letter or a syllable or word-cluster to explore the densities, measures, weights, textures, sounds, movements, sights & silences in the body & skin that is language - and being open to, dwelling in, & turning inside-out – figuring out the word in all its multiform abrasions, magnetisms, beauties & musics & incertitudes too.

In a restrictive culture where the dominance of notions of poetry are centred around the referential, transparent axis, such working with the material matter of language is highly subversive. I'll leave the last eloquent words to Tom Leonard, with whom I utterly concur:

It's not simply a matter of class register, but the politics of dominant narrative language as would-be encloser of the world, language as coloniser. For this the language has to be presumed 'invisible' to its referent. I like to make it visible in different ways.

Don Paterson

*What's going on in contemporary poetry that interests you? Is poetry in a
healthy state at the moment, or is it heading nowhere?*

The tree's flourishing, which is good, as poetry was criminally underpublished
in the seventies and early eighties; but I think we've gone far too far in the
opposite direction now. A bit of severe pruning's long overdue. I *can't* believe
that there are more than 30 books of poems worth publishing each year; if you
do a quick *per capita*, even America comes nowhere near the UK – yet
overproduction is proverbial in relation to the American poetry scene. We
suffer from the delusion that this country is far larger than it really is, and that
poetry is a far less marginal activity than it really is. It's just not possible that
that many people are very good at it, but as long as we go on putting the accent
on creative writing rather than creative reading, that's always going to be the
way of it. But overpublication's a serious problem, as it just makes the good
stuff all the harder for the casual or innocent reader to get to. There are some
fine poets around, though I don't think we're quite in a golden age. I suspect
many of the great 'individual voices', the terminal ironies and the piddling
concerns of this generation are going to look very tired and embarrassing in 50
years time.

*What chances and risks are taken in your own work, or the work you have
edited/published?*

In terms of the authors or books I've edited, I don't think I've taken any risks
at all, but I would say that, wouldn't I... I have this old-fashioned view that a
poet is someone with the gift of composing verses, and I'd like to think that all
the authors on the Picador list fall into that category. I'd also be quite worried
if that statement didn't provoke some disagreement, otherwise it'd be a sign
you were involved in some sort of consensus publishing. You publish a book
out of enthusiasm or admiration.

How does your writing inform your work as an editor?

Editing doesn't help my writing one bit; all you're doing is dredging up bits of
machinery that normally sit below the waterline of conscious operation, then
taking them to bits, pointing and poking at them... so it's harder for you to go
back to your own stuff and be unselfconscious and instinctive about it all again,
metrics and all the finer points of versification... You could easily end up like
a paranoid aircraft engineer, having lost so much of his innocent faith in the
machine that he's too scared ever to get in a plane again.

What processes lie behind the writing of your poems? Are you prolific? How often do you write? How much editing and rewriting goes into your own poetry?

I'm not prolific at all; half a dozen poems a year, at the moment, though some might be pretty long. The amount of drafting involved is just embarrassing; I suppose I'm trying to achieve a kind of poem-as-formal-system, well-designed enough not to need me around to help it, to act as its parent or apologist or whatever... Like those watches you just have to shake a little to wind up again.

What important influences have shaped your current interests? What are you reading at present?

I'm reading very little poetry – I feel I've read too much of the stuff, anyway. Sometimes it seems the more you read the more your little private canon dwindles, but maybe that's no bad thing; maybe that's the truth of it. I think reading lots of poetry can be counterproductive for a poet; there are many other things that are far more likely to stimulate your imagination, especially if you edit the stuff.

Hybrids & Collaborations...?

Poetry's the most untransformable, intractable medium of the lot, I think, so it always suffers when it's dragged into another. Collaboration's different, though – I've done some quite satisfying things when I've managed to keep the whole creative process fluid right up to the end – that way it's proper collaboration, not mere co-operation, which is what the poet usually has to settle for, handing over his or her poem and letting the composer or artist do their worst. But if you can develop a *modus operandi* that involves you both right up to the end, it'll allow you to take advantage of all the little serendipitous things and happy accidents that any process will throw up – if you can't do that, then a process simply isn't enjoyable. It also allows you the flexibility to work round all the *unhappy* accidents, which is just as important. I did a little poem-film with my friend Rupert Jones; I had a rough draft, but totally rewrote the poem in the editing suite to fit the funny things he had shot, and he worked round me in the same way. I'm working with the composer Gordon McPherson on a full-length melodrama in a similar fashion. I think the trick is to realise that a hybrid form, if it has any integrity at all, must develop its own rules and strategies, and that you can't simply import the old ones and expect them to have the same force or validity. The other trick is to remember that what's an innovation in one medium is, more often than not, already a cliché in another. Anything that strikes you as a brilliant idea almost certainly isn't.

How do you select work for a poetry list/anthology? Should poetry lists/ anthologies demonstrate consistency, or diversity?

A list should demonstrate diversity, absolutely, and I'd have no hesitation in publishing work I admired but didn't personally like. The danger is unconsciously remaking a list in your own image; I can think of lists where this has happened in the past – I'm sure we all can. For example, knowing that I do have a bias towards formal verse, I probably make far more of an effort than I would do otherwise to look out for stuff that's not like that at all. Sometimes that unusual thing happens, and you're just blown away and convinced that the world will be a better place for the publication of such and such book. I suppose I felt that when I read Billy Collins. But at the end of the day there's only one way an editor ever chooses a poet: educated whim. Inevitably that'll lead to a list formed partly by their prejudices and tastes, there's no way round that. It's unsatisfactory, but there's no alternative. All you can do is stay alert to it, listen to people, try and act responsibly.

Should poetry be difficult, or should poets make their work easily understandable?

Poets shouldn't be self-conscious about the 'difficulty' of their poetry, that's the only rule. Otherwise they find themselves second-guessing an audience, and writing poems that are wilfully obscure or wilfully accessible, and readers – even if they're too instinctive to appreciate anything else – always recognise inauthenticity. Poets are forever sitting round talking about making some decent money by writing a Mills and Boon or something – but they can't do it; they'd always be self-consciously writing down, and even readers of pulp romances would see that immediately.

Is there a 'new poetry'? What is it?

No, there isn't a new poetry; anyone who thinks they're writing one hasn't read the old stuff. The more superficially innovative a poem is, the more quickly it seems brings to mind something that's already been done.

Given that poetry in general falls short of audience numbers & big book sales, what should be the motivating forces of poetry publishing?

Several things: from the publisher's point of view, poetry gives teeth to the list, lends it a seriousness of literary intent; from the editor's – if you're going to be Buddhist about it, all you're doing is playing midwife to good poetry, so you should take as much pleasure in publishing other folk's stuff as your own, as it amounts to the same act. It's a very singular high, too: I mean I've gotten such a kick out of how well Paul Farley's done.

Is contemporary poetry a divided thing? Divided which ways? How are you bridging the gaps?

I think it is divided, and we can do a lot to bridge the gaps by a) ignoring them, and b) ignoring the people who make it their business to widen them.

How do you feel about the devices that are used to divide poetry up into schools? As an editor, what are you doing to combat this?

I confess, I have no interest in schools whatsoever. Anyone affiliating themselves with a school only does so through a lack of confidence to go it alone, but as a transitional phase, it probably does some poets a lot of good; you just have to know when you've graduated. Again, that lack of understanding between bits of the poetry world... I don't think it's worth addressing; the only really serious schism is between 'page poetry' and performance poetry, and the gap is closing as, perversely, the two sides recognise that they're playing very different games – so they can learn from each other, rather than compete. The only other one I can think of is that Cambridge lot and the rest of the world, but they have no interest in finding a readership. A shame, because some of them are really talented, but any agenda that doesn't consider the poem to be a kind of performance before a reader, a *non-practising* reader, is soon going to become hopelessly warped. When you actually get one of these poets on their own, it turns out they espouse all the same virtues of lyricism, clarity and concision that you do, only they've contrived to find them in Prynne and not in Heaney. It just shows you what happens when you shut up a lot of very clever people in a room. Exactly the same thing that happened this century to Oxford philosophy when it went down the linguistic analysis road, all that talk about talk about talk.

Do you see any heirarchies of publishing as existing at present?

Yes, there *are* hierarchies, and shouldn't be. Hierarchies should just be about who's got the best poets, but just about all the major lists have major poets. Alas, one or two of the subsidised lists publish far too much, so *their* major poets don't get a look in. Until it becomes a condition of their subsidy to publish ten books a year and spend the rest of the money on marketing and distribution, things are going to be quite impossible for many of their authors.

Why do some poets choose to operate from within the small press only?

I'm afraid it's a complete fantasy that poets *choose* to operate within the small presses. I've yet to meet one poet who wouldn't jump ship to a commercial list at the first opportunity, whatever they might say on the record. The exceptions are Les Murray at Carcanet, and Carol Ann Duffy, who's demonstrated a remarkable loyalty to Anvil, though she's been published by commercial lists too. I find that very admirable, if a little quixotic.

What are your interests regarding questions of sexual politics & gender in poetry?

I have little interest in gender issues, except to say I can see no reason why a list should eventually have anything other than an equal number of male and female poets. I mean how could it possibly work out any other way? To even start addressing some aspects of the 'gender question' seriously seems to be dignifying many issues long since rendered non-issues through the irresistible arguments of feminists in the seventies and eighties. There is a still a serious problem, true, with poetry editors; they're all blokes. It'll change, but it was always going to be the last thing to change. Things always have to change at a social level first, and that's beginning to happen as the gender-composition of the lists starts to even up; it's just a matter of lunch, really. Once we get lunch sorted out then everything else will follow. But I admit it's painfully slow.

What are your interests re: social politics in poetry?

The publication of poetry is a political gesture in itself, as far as I'm concerned, a liberal and democratic one. The quality of that gesture's up to the poet, though.

How do you feel about the 'Anthology Wars'; the editorial arguments surrounding many post-war British anthologies?

I think the 'anthology wars' at least served to give the journalists something to write about; in our recent Penguin v. Picador spat, both books ended up getting more coverage than they would have managed if it they'd come out six months apart. Some people seemed to think that the degree of concurrence in their contents was a bit sinister. I thought that was ridiculous: both books went out of their way to be inclusive, and I know for a fact that all the editors involved included work they didn't personally like. Quite right too: it was about access and the broad church, not canon-formation. You can't form canons in contemporary work and claim them to be anything other than utterly subjective selections. One of the good things about these anthologies is that, apart from their usefulness as general introductions, they go some way to correcting the injustices that are inevitably visited upon the 'mainstream' by individual (male) editors running the lists on personal whim. So let's have more of them. I mean I thought Ian Sinclair's *Conductors of Chaos* was mostly terrible work, but it was nonetheless very important that that book came out with a commercial publisher. And it's sold pretty well, actually.

Why still publish books in the 'electronic age'?

We'll go on publishing books because they're such a perfect design – lovely, analogue, human-shaped things, like wrist-watches. I mean who wears a digital watch, now? We realised that the old design couldn't be improved upon. It was aesthetically more satisfying, truer, more human. I don't doubt that digital technology will influence book design in the future, but not very radically.

Are you interested in electronic publishing? Which e-journals/discussion lists/ poetry websites do you use?

Yes, I'm very interested in electronic publishing; not just the dissemination of material already printed in book form, but all the I think the use of interactive stuff, hypertext linking and what have you. I'm sure it'll eventually spawn a form of poetry quite distinct and new. It won't supersede the old one, but I'm sure there'll be a lot of fruitful cross-fertilisation in the future.

Deryn Rees-Jones

What important influences have shaped your current interests? What are you reading at present?

The biggest influence on my work has been my reading of feminist theory. I certainly wouldn't define myself as a theorist, but feminist thinking and philosophy – sexual politics, gender, sexuality and psychoanalysis – is something which excites me. I wrote my doctoral thesis on post-war women's poetry and women's anxiety about how to configure the female 'I', and how surrealism is a good technique for simultaneously masking and displaying concerns about the self. Luce Irigaray is probably the writer who interests me the most. I don't read her to 'believe her', but to stimulate me, to make me think. Also, what she writes about angels in relation to gender has proved important to the work I'm doing in *Consorting With Angels*, my book of essays on modern women poets. But I also like Julia Kristeva. She can be an incredibly moving writer. One of the awful things about writing a thesis is the way it narrows your thinking, obsessively so. My partner is writing a thesis on poetry and exile, and is interested in Eastern European poetry, and photography. So there is a constant filtering in of his interests into what I'm reading or thinking. And of course I'm an academic who teaches Creative Writing, so there is a steady drip of influences from my students. But what you seem to lose by working in a profession concerned with literature is that intense excitement of discovery you get when you're a teenager, desperate to read and to have the world opened up. With discernment and a stronger recognition of your own taste inevitably comes dissatisfaction, and disappointment.

At the moment I'm reading the *Beginners Guide to Quantum Theory* and Jonathon Dollimore's *Death, Desire and Loss in Western Culture*. I've just started *The Magic Mountain* which I've been meaning to read for about 10 years, John Burnside's novel *The Mercy Boys* (which has an angel in the very first chapter!) and just finished Patricia Duncker's collection of short stories, *Monsieur Shoushana's Lemon Trees*. I'm a huge fan of her novel *Hallucinating Foucault*.

Poets I admire? Donne, Smart, Whitman, Neruda, Lorca, Muldoon, Lowell, Hughes, Gunn, Plath, Bishop. I like early Medbh McGuckian, Michael Donaghy, Jo Shapcott. I also very much admire the work of Gwyneth Lewis, Matt Simpson, Maurice Riordan. Although they are very different poets they all write with absolute integrity – Gwyneth Lewis I like for her formal qualities and her use of the sequence, Matt Simpson for managing a kind of gritty lyricism, Maurice Riordan for his ability to wrestle with and expand on ideas, and for his understatement. Other poets I admire are Carol Ann Duffy, George Szirtes, Anne Stevenson, Denise Riley, John Burnside, Elizabeth Jennings. One thing that did happen when I was writing the thesis was that I read very little written by men, and although that was probably necessary at the time, I feel I have a lot of catching up to do.

Since then, I've been writing *Consorting with Angels*, so reading women's poetry has become part of work, rather than part of my personal reading, though of course it's hard to divide the two. The idea of that book is to show the ways in which women's poetry does interact, refigure, redefine poetry written by their male and often canonical contemporaries or influences.

Are you interested in hybridizing poetries, or hybridizing poetry with other art forms?

I think you have to be careful. Hybrids can be incredibly beautiful and stimulating, but they can also be dangerously rootless, somehow, and sterile. I am certainly interested in ways in which other art forms, music and art can help me think about the way in which I write. I find listening to twentieth century music frustrating, challenging, difficult. I still would rather listen to Mozart or Haydn, or Bach. My partner listens to a lot of music, and slowly I'm learning to appreciate it, but it takes a lot of patience! Webern, for example, makes me instinctively want to pull my hair out, but I'm learning to take small bites. Listening to the pianist Joanna MacGregor has really helped me to think about music in a different way: she is, for example, very interested in cross-overs between contemporary music and jazz, and she talks about what she plays in a way that is inspiring. Through her I've discovered Charles Ives and Django Bates. I would certainly like to think that learning about musical form, even in the most rudimentary way, has contributed to the way I think about my poetry, and in particular about the way in which you assemble a book of poems.

I find I can appreciate modern and contemporary art much more easily than music, and again I think I have fairly eclectic tastes. I really like the work of Dorothy Cross, Paula Rego, Ana Maria Pacheco, Shani Rhys James. We have a print of an upside-down cup and saucer by the Scottish artist Merilyn Smith over our fireplace at home. It's wonderful! Incredibly disturbing to have this really simple object, which, taken out of any spatial context and inverted, becomes a very shocking image.

But going back to this hybridity question, I don't necessarily think that the cross-over has to be with other art forms. Merilyn was talking recently about a piece which she did in Liverpool in 1984, *Helix aspera sublima Smith*. She painted two hundred and fifty snails with brilliant enamels and put them in the quadrangle of the Bluecoat Chambers garden. The project was researched meticulously to ensure the snails' safety, and Merilyn collaborated a great deal with specialists at the universities in Edinburgh, Manchester and St. Andrews. The scientists were really interested in this from a scientific point of view, and wanted her to publish the research in scientific journals. That seems to me a really interesting way of combining specialisms to create something interesting and beautiful.

Thinking about other people's work does, of course, make you question your own work. And I'm fairly sure that slowly the infiltration of ideas will change the way I think – or rather consolidate and develop my own work. I'm always wondering how would I do that as a poet? How could I do that in words? What would its equivalent be? I don't know that I come up with many answers!

We are starting a Masters degree in Creative Arts at Liverpool Hope where I work, and the aspect I'm co-ordinating is in 'Writing and Reading Poetry'. At the moment this gives writing students the chance to work with members of the music department, and what I'm hoping is that this will expand to include collaborations with the art department too. It doesn't have to stop there, however, and maybe there'll be a chance for some interdisciplinary work between arts and sciences in the future.

Should poetry be difficult, or should poets make their work easily understandable?

That question does depend on so many things. It assumes that the seemingly simple can't be complex. Blake is a case in point. It also depends what you mean by understandable – and to whom. Just because I don't understand a language that doesn't necessarily mean that I'm excluded through difficulty. I'm excluded because I don't have, or wasn't taught, the language. So a big part of it comes down to education. I'm certainly interested in complexity. But when was anything worthwhile easily understandable? That does assume we understand in a purely literal way. What's difficult for me may not be difficult for someone else. And vice versa!

What are your interests regarding questions of sexual politics in gender and poetry?

I'm very interested in exploring gender in my work: an engagement with feminist thinking informs critical and creative work and of course the two feed into each other. I remember when I was a student I went to what, in retrospect, was quite a high- powered writing group that was very much dictated by a very rigourous kind of new critical analysis of poems that we brought to the group. At the time I was writing these clear, imagist, completely unsexed poems:

adhering to all Pound's hard, dry maxims (his imagist manifestos are something I still use as kind of touchstone, especially when I'm teaching poetry).

I remember one afternoon particularly because, at the coffee break, a young man benevolently said to me that he hoped I wasn't going to write any of those awful women's poems. I think it was meant to be some kind of back-handed compliment, but my feelings about that comment have dictated an awful lot of my thinking about women and poetry since then. How does one analyse a comment like that: as a 'helpful' pointer to continue to write in as ungendered a way as possible? To write well, to write like men? To not write about things which destabilise, embarrass, threaten the status quo?

Certainly, thinking of one's self simply and always as a woman is restricting and restrictive. I've just finished teaching a poetry class to women on a Women's Studies M.A. Many of the women hadn't written since they were at school, and yet within seven weeks they were finding a voice, beginning to find a confidence with language and with ways of talking about particular experiences. I'm really glad that the women on this course have a chance to explore their own creativity alongside their knowledge of the criminal justice system, psychology, race, gender, feminist theory, class; I want to provide them with an atmosphere in which they can write about experiences which are difficult, important in a history of women's struggles; but I don't want to reduce their creativity to simply an exploration of their experience or their experience of oppression. Nor do I want them not to read poetry by men: even if sometimes that poetry positions them in an unpleasant way. I want them to read good poetry, that stretches language, imagination, perception, and then write their own: this seems to me the only way to resist positioning in this way. It's necessary to develop an ability to explore male and female experience in a more interesting way that misogyny, for example, ever can. Resisting dominant or even residual feelings about male/female relations can't ever come through a denigration of the masculine per se, but through presenting alternative images of women and men in a way which is useful and aesthetically interesting.

I do ask myself frequently whether women's poetry is different from that written by men; whether it is as technically able; whether it does actually fall into a stereotyped divide, in that women's poetry feels through language, whereas men's poetry attempts to display a mastery of language. But I also think that until women poets are written about, and put to that test, they never will be able to develop as individuals within a powerful literary tradition. This isn't from a lack of ambition or ability, but because of the eradicated nature of women's literary history where the struggle is obliterated or marginalised or made eccentric. I do believe that at its best criticism sends one back to the text it is exploring: more alive to its possibilities, its capabilities.

I am very much aware of my debt to women poets who write now and wrote before me. I also believe that, in spite of the number of poets writing today, few are of any great stature; few are women. These ideas of greatness are not ones that obsess me. What does is a sense of complacency about the fact that women's poetry is here to stay; that the many poets writing today won't be remembered and catalogued in future accounts of poetry at the end of the twentieth century. Maybe that displays an undue pessimism; it's not a desire to conserve for conservation's sake, but grows from an awareness of how many periods of writing activity there have been, and women whose work was popular, widely read, and which then disappeared from the canon.

Do we need anthologies which divide poets thematically/stylistically/politically/ gender wise?

Yes, and no. The question that this one begs is, of course, why do we need anthologies. I think most poets have secret mental anthologies of poems that they refer to consciously or unconsciously throughout their lives. I think too often the criteria for selection becomes too influenced by publishing or political dimensions. Demands of the market, that sort of thing. I was very pleased to have been included in *Making for Planet Alice*, and it was nice to have an anthology named after one of my poems. But I am curious about the way in which I was represented in that book: curious about the way in which the choices are made. I don't think the poems included actually show me at my best, or perhaps at my most complex. They don't really represent a version of myself I'd recognise.

The book I have edited for Macmillan with my friend Alison Mark, *Contemporary Women's Poetry: Reading/Writing/Practice*, brings together the work of poets and critics: some poets who write as critics, some about the process of their own writing. There is hardly any critical writing on contemporary women's poetry in Britain and Ireland, and this book aims to bring together British, Irish and American poets and to look at them in relation to each other, while also placing the work of more experimental writers alongside more mainstream poets. If women's work is marginalised in the mainstream, then that is even more the case in avant-garde writing. Bringing together twenty-one women writers, one of the points is not to show similarities but to show differences, disputes, as well as connections and places of exchange. So we have women critics writing about women poets, women poets writing criticism about women poets, and women poets writing about themselves. If I edited anything again I'd like to bring together men and women to write on women's poetry – maybe that's the next project... We've also talked about editing an anthology of women's poetry since 1900 that could be used as a teaching anthology. One thing I'm sure of, however, is that at the moment I'm spending too much energy writing about poetry and not writing it, or even having the luxury of researching or reading as preparation for writing it.

Contributors' Notes

TIM ALLEN is the editor of www.terriblework.co.uk. His publications are *Texts for a Holy Saturday* (Phlebas) and *The Cruising Duct* (Maquette). His work appears in magazines including *Oasis* and *Shearsman*. He is currently editing a book of online interviews with poets, with Andrew Duncan for Salt Publications.

GILLIAN ALLNUTT was Poetry Editor at *City Limits* from 1983 to 1988. She also co-edited *The New British Poetry* (Paladin). Her collections are *Spitting the Pips Out* (Sheba), *Beginning the Avocado* (Virago), *Blackthorn*, *Nantucket and the Angel* and *Lintel* (each Bloodaxe), shortlisted for the T.S. Eliot Prize. She is the author of *Berthing: A Poetry Workbook* (National Extension College/Virago) and has held two RLF Fellowships.

NEIL ASTLEY is editor of Bloodaxe Books. He has edited several anthologies including *Staying Alive* (Bloodaxe / Miramax), *Poetry with an Edge*, *New Blood*, *Pleased to See Me* and *Do Not Go Gentle* (all Bloodaxe). His own collections are *Darwin Survivor* and *Biting My Tongue*. He has published a critical book on Tony Harrison and a novel, *The End of My Tether*, shortlisted for the Whitbread First Novel Award in 2002.

CAROLINE BERGVALL is Associate Research Fellow in Performance Writing at Dartington College of Arts and Associate Writer in Creative Writing at Cardiff University. Her books include *Eclat* (Sound&Language), *Goan Atom*, and *1: Doll* (Krupskaya). Her work includes audio texts and collaborative performances and installations with artists, most recently *Figs, 1, 2, 3* (South London Gallery).

TILLA BRADING is assistant editor of *Poetry Quarterly Review*. Her most recent published works are *Autumnal Jour* (Maquette) and *Notes In The Manor: Of Speaking* (Leafe Press). Her work appears widely in poetry journals and in exhibitions. She teaches freelance Creative Writing and is assistant Custodian of Coleridge Cottage.

ANDY BROWN is Lecturer in Creative Writing & Arts at the University of Exeter, and was a Centre Director for the Arvon Foundation. He has published four collections, *Hunting the Kinnayas* (Stride), *From A Cliff* (Arc), *The Wanderer's Prayer* (Arc) and *West of Yesterday* (Stride). He writes and publishes short fiction and is editing an anthology of new lyric poets and a book of critical essays.

JOHN BURNSIDE teaches Creative Writing and Literature and Ecology at the University of St. Andrews. His most recent books of poems are *The*

Light Trap and *The Asylum Dance* (both Cape), which won the Whitbread Prize for Poetry. He is also a novelist, whose most recent novels are *The Mercy Boys, The Locust Room* and *Living Nowhere* (Cape). A new poetry collection, *The Good Neighbour*, is planned for early 2005.

RICHARD CADDEL was a librarian in Durham University and a founding director of the Basil Bunting Poetry Centre. He edited Bunting's *Complete Poems* (OUP) and *OTHER: British and Irish Poetry Since 1970* (Wesleyan). His own poems include *Uncertain Time* (Galloping Dog), *Larksong Signal* (Shearsman) and the Selected, *Magpie Words* (Westhouse Books). Richard Caddel died in 2002.

MILES CHAMPION's books include *Sore Models* (Sound & Language) and *Three Bell Zero* (Roof Books). *Air Ball* (with Trevor Winkfield) is forthcoming from Tolling Elves in 2004. Born in Nottingham, England, he currently lives in New York City.

CRIS CHEEK is a poet-pedagogue, writer-critic, book artist-publisher, new media practitioner and interdisciplinary performer. His writing has been commissioned and shown widely, often in multiple versions using diverse media. His work is increasingly site-responsive and frequently created in full collaboration with other artists, most notably with Kirsten Lavers as TNWK.

MICHAEL DONAGHY's collections to date are *Shibboleth* (OUP), *Errata* (OUP), *Dances Learned Last Night: Poems 1975-1995* (Picador) and *Conjure* (Picador). He has won the Forward Prize, the Whitbread Prize for Poetry and the Geoffrey Faber Prize. He teaches poetry workshops at City University and Birkbeck College and is a Fellow of The Royal Society of Literature.

KEN EDWARDS' books include the poetry collections *Intensive Care*, *Good Science*, *3600 Weekends*, *eight + six*, and the novel *Futures*. He has been editor/publisher of Reality Street Editions since 1993. He is active in music as well as writing, including his text for a piece by John Tilbury for piano, voice and sampled sounds, *There's Something in There*.

PETER FINCH is a poet, experimental performer and Director of the Welsh Academi. In the 60s and 70s he edited the groundbreaking magazine *second aeon*. He has published over two dozen collections of poetry including *Selected Poems* (Poetry Wales), *Useful* (Seren) and *Antibodies* (Stride). His web site is at http://dspace.dial.pipex.com/peter.finch. He is the author of *Real Cardiff* (Seren). His *Selected Poems* in Hungarian translation, *Vizet* (*Water*), appears this year.

JANET FISHER lives in Huddersfield, where she is the co-director of The Poetry Business with Peter Sansom. Her collections are *Listening to Dancing* (Smith/Doorstop) and *Women Who Dye Their Hair* (Smith/Doorstop).

LINDA FRANCE has published four collections with Bloodaxe Books. The latest is *The Simultaneous Dress*. She edited the anthology *Sixty Women Poets* (Bloodaxe). Her verse biography of 18th century writer and traveller Lady Mary Wortley Montagu, *The Toast of the Kit Cat Club*, is due from Bloodaxe in 2004. She is currently working on her first novel.

DAVID KENNEDY's most recent publications are *The President of Earth* (Salt) and *C: A Circuition Around His Circumambulation* (West House). He was a co-editor of *The New Poetry* (Bloodaxe) and the author of *New Relations: The Refashioning of British Poetry 1980-1994* (Seren).

JOHN KINSELLA's most recent book is *Peripheral Light: Selected and New Poems* (Norton). He is a Fellow of Churchill College, Cambridge, and Professor of English at Kenyon College, Ohio.

RUPERT LOYDELL is currently an RLF Project Fellow and a Visiting Fellow at Warwick University. He is Reviews Editor of *Orbis* magazine and Managing Editor of Stride Publications. His most recent books are *The Museum of Light* (Arc) and *Endlessly Divisible* (Driftwood).

SARAH MAGUIRE's most recent collection of poems is *The Florist's at Midnight* (Cape). She edited *Flora Poetica: The Chatto Book of Botanical Verse* (Chatto & Windus). Her selected poems, *Haleeb Muraq*, was translated by the distinguished Iraqi poet, Saadi Yousef, and published in Damascus in 2003. She teaches poetry translation at The School of Oriental and African Studies, London.

DAVID MORLEY is Director of the Warwick Writing Programme and the author of the collection *Scientific Papers* (Carcanet). He has received a major Gregory Award, a Tyrone Guthrie Award from Northern Arts, a Hawthornden Fellowship, an Arts Council Writers Award and an Arts Council Fellowship in Writing. He co-edited *The New Poetry* for Bloodaxe and in 2002 edited *The Gift*, an anthology of new writing for the NHS.

SHEILA E. MURPHY is a US poet and visual artist. *Letters to Unfinished J.*, the 2001 winner of the Gertrude Stein Poetry Award, has just appeared from Green Integer. *Green Tea with Ginger* is recently released from Potes & Poets Press. Murphy was co-founder and co-ordinator of the Scottsdale Center for the Arts Poetry Series.

MAGGIE O'SULLIVAN edited *Out of Everywhere: linguistically innovative poetry by women in North America and the UK* (Reality Street Editions). Her published works include *Unofficial Word* (Galloping Dog), *In The House of the Shaman* (Reality Street Editions) and *Palace of Reptiles* (Sun & Moon).

DON PATERSON works as a musician and editor; he also teaches Creative Writing at the University of St Andrews. His highly commended collections are *Nil Nil*, *God's Gift to Women*, *The Eyes* and *Landing Light* (all Faber). The recipient of the T.S. Eliot Prize and the Geoffrey Faber Memorial Prize, he lives in Kirriemuir, Angus.

DERYN REES-JONES lectures in English at the University of Liverpool. Her books of poetry are *The Memory Tray* and *Signs Round a Dead Body* (both Seren). Her book-length poem *Quiver: A Mystery* is published by Seren in 2004.

EVA SALZMAN's books are *The English Earthquake* (Bloodaxe), *Bargain with the Watchman* (OUP), *One Two II* (Wrecking Ball Press) and *Double Crossing: New and Selected Poems* (Bloodaxe). She was West Midlands Writing Fellow at Warwick University and is currently Royal Literary Fund Project Fellow at Ruskin College, Oxford.